AN AMERICAN
DIVORCE

J N Welch

Author: Anonymous

Copyright c 2019 by William H. Honaker, The IP Guy.

CONTENTS

J. N. Welch

Chapter 1: Going Back to College

When two people decide to get a divorce, it isn't that they don't understand one another, but a sign that they have, at last, begun to.

—Helen Rowland

Although the White male receives very little respect in today's political climate, there was a time when the reverse was true. After centuries of medieval kings, popes, and serfs, a handful of European intellectuals found themselves on the cusp of overturning an entire global order. The sixteenth-century Protestant reformers rejected the mystical powers of the pope; logic would thus follow—the "king" was nothing more than a mere mortal as well. And if the pope and the king had no direct link to God, then reason would suggest there was no intermediary between man and his almighty Creator.

Envision this new way of thinking colliding with a distant land, free from the medieval baggage associated with Europe and Asia. The ultimate plan was dependent on White males with property to resist voting for politicians who were corrupt, inept, or both. From this democratic foundation, a newly discovered land would attract risk-averse human beings from every continent on the planet—and those millions of human

5

beings were liberated from the shackles of tyrants, monarchs, and warlords.

These circumstances explain how the US became an exceptional country. An unpolluted land essentially collided with a transcendent set of ideas. Today, of course, there is no longer glory in the American founding. The United States is drowning in guilt, division, and apathy. To the progressive elites, the US is merely a sham that left out slaves, women, and natives. Forget the fact that taking arbitrary power away from a monarch was one of the biggest gambles in human history. In today's "cancel culture" the Founding Fathers were simply privileged scoundrels whose monuments and namesakes should be removed and destroyed. The United States has become the once-beautiful supermodel who can only see ugliness and imperfection when she peers into a mirror.

All of us can feel the division and dysfunction, but we don't know where to begin the conversation. When the US experienced divorce in the 1860s, most Americans understood what the breakup was ultimately about. Today, things are not quite as simple. We're not listening to Stephen Douglas and Abraham Lincoln lay out dueling platforms with moral and intellectual clarity. In today's *fascist* environment, careers are lost and reputations are destroyed overnight simply for saying the wrong thing to the wrong person. And anyone who dares to challenge the conventional wisdom of the elites is deemed to be an unenlightened lightweight, or even a personal threat, to those select groups who meet today's politically correct criteria of being "disadvantaged." In a world with big problems and complex challenges, we are often left with these types of academic questions at many of our prized universities:

• Should disadvantaged college students be afforded "safe zones" to feel more comfortable in their well-being?

- Should human beings even continue using words like "man" and "woman?" Or should gender identity be a fluid and individual choice?
- Do White people understand that their consciousness is flawed because of privilege?

The United States of America has come full circle as a civilization. The country that was first to walk away from authoritarian rule is, today, powerless to confront the tyranny found in its own back yard.

I grew up in a lower/middle-income neighborhood. My politics were first influenced by my grandfather's love of Franklin Roosevelt and John F. Kennedy. On Sunday mornings, we would listen to FDR's fireside chats on those old LP albums. I still find emotion in the charisma and confidence both presidents displayed during some very difficult times in America. After graduating from high school, I went off to college. Thirty-seven years later, though, I can still remember the first spoken words from an early morning philosophy class. After strolling into class late, the professor carefully scanned the room and declared, *"Boy, it's colder than a nun's cunt outside!"*

Later in that same class, he proclaimed:

All of you are being held in intellectual shackles. Your parents may be nice people, but they are simply pawns—tending to their lawns, obeying their bosses, and raising their flags on patriotic holidays. You, on the other hand, are going to have an opportunity your parents never had; you're going to find liberation from the hypocrisy and illusion of what America really stands for.

We all have that moment in life when we first contemplate our parents are not perfect. I still remember going home from college after that first day and looking down on my mom and dad. I felt sorry for them and their simple ways.

Several years later, I quit college to take over a failing family business. I was no longer in the theoretical environment of a classroom and soon began to realize my parents weren't the simpletons the philosophy instructor had first led me to believe. I was working on construction crews and quickly got a taste of life outside the classroom. Whether one lives near a city such as Oakland, Baltimore, or Cleveland, most of us have become immune to a local news cycle almost certain to begin with an overnight smash-and-grab, abduction, or homicide. Unfortunately, I saw the harsh reality of inner-city life on the first day of the job. While riding up an elevator in a public housing complex, I stood side-by-side as the elevator attendant and a building occupant got into a knife fight.

And the fun didn't end in the elevator. In the suburbs where I grew up, random women would never proposition me into their apartments for sex. In that HUD facility, however, every day would feature the same morning routine. As I walked through the halls with other crewmembers, women would stand in front of their doorways, asking the younger guys to come inside for a "quickie." Many of these women had no qualms with their openness, while four or five children stood behind them in the doorway.

Before college, I had never seen a house on fire. In the low-rent districts, however, it wasn't uncommon to see one or two houses burning every week.

And to this day, if you're not careful picking the right gas station beyond the heavily policed areas, there is a reasonable chance you will become the next statistic from a violent carjacking.

After spending a decade going through the normal ebb and flow associated with growing a business, I decided to return to the university to finish what I couldn't complete in the 1980s. I spent the next twenty years as an adult listening to the same drumbeat I first heard out of high school. I began college when Ronald Reagan was president and graduated when Barack Obama was two years into his presidency. In what could best be explained as a Rodney Dangerfield, *Back to School* experience, it was fascinating to begin a day downtown and then finish the evening in an academic setting with progressive *intellectuals*. To the professors, of course, every urban problem was cleverly displaced back to White privilege, income inequality, and racism. Forget the fact I rarely saw fathers in any of those housing complexes. And forget the reality that many urban areas in the US look like a Mad Max setting of dilapidated housing, abandoned automobiles, and random dump sites. Those anecdotal observations simply had little relevance to any classroom discussion that didn't begin with *racism* and end with *privilege*.

I spent three decades sitting through a cult-like experience, and I understand the progressive mindset as if it were my own. There were even times when I would use their playbook to question my own belief systems:

- Was my conservative bent influenced by *privilege*?
- Did my experience as a construction worker make my masculinity *toxic*?
- Did my experiences in inner-city HUD projects make me a *racist*?

Today, both the political left and right seem to agree on one thing: America is going downhill quickly. The left attributes the decline to massive inequality, too much power in the hands of corporations, and a planet on the verge of overheating. The

9

right sees a country where its people have lost their moral and competitive edge to do great things. One side views the human existence as a continual struggle against egotism and evil, while the other questions whether concepts like "evil" still have a place in the modern world. There is one side that wishes to return to the good old days and another side that views traditional America as a model of hypocrisy, designed primarily to serve the interests of privileged White people. Both groups are entrenched in the politics of mutual destruction.

Our twenty-first-century intellectuals do have an impressive ledger of scholarly distinctions, and they know how to solve complex problems on paper. They have come to believe they are intellectually enlightened, and that Republican voters are a combination of racists, religious crazies, greedy millionaires and billionaires, or those who are dumb enough to vote for a president who lies every day. There are reasons why today's elites take themselves so seriously and view all dissenters with such disdain. The progressive mind of the twenty-first century carries the tremendous burden of shepherding the world's inhabitants out of a *tribal* mindset that has plagued humanity since the dawn of time. They are also working diligently in an era of globalization to protect the masses from bourgeois exploitation—and to make matters even more profound today—their sense of purpose is in a frantic state to rescue the planet.

For years, the conventional wisdom of most parents was to find any way to send the kids off to college. This method still works for those students who have the smarts and work ethic to become doctors, scientists, and engineers. But not many American kids have what it takes to get into the physical sciences, nor do they have what it takes to perform strenuous labor. So, our high school graduates gravitate to the "cupcake" majors in college, and this is where the indoctrination begins.

Today, there are millions of millennials who view each personal failure through the lens of a perpetual struggle as a victim. Every hardship in life can be easily projected back onto capitalism, sexism, or racism. Every problem in the world can be intellectually displaced onto millionaires and billionaires, including the billions of dollars in student-debt loans tied to a piece of paper that has very little value in today's global economy.

The mindset of perpetual victimhood represents a beautiful psychology for those revolutionary leaders who know how to use the leftist playbook. There are millions of clueless *adults* who will go through life trying to merge personal inadequacies into a life-changing movement that seeks to find greater levels of *empathy, equality, and social justice*. Bernie Sanders was an unaccomplished loner in Congress. Yet, Sanders could have easily won the US presidency in both 2016 and 2020. Sanders's success was most reflected in the sheer number of millennials who bought into the same regurgitated nonsense I first heard at the university in the 1980s. True to Marxist form, Sanders was able to project individual fear and insecurity onto a billionaire bogeyman.

It is true this type of talk will come across as insensitive to those younger Americans who have bought into the logic that millionaires and billionaires are responsible for every problem in the world. Many college-educated millennials are oblivious to the cultural reality that lies beyond the ivy-covered university walls, the travel-abroad cities, and the watchful eyes of the local police departments. When US students visit Paris, they go to the Louvre or the Eiffel Tower. They are not walking through the backstreets of Seine-Saint-Denis. And when the kids go to Chicago for a weekend road trip, they're attending a Lollapalooza concert at Grant Park. They are not taking a stroll through the bad neighborhoods of Fuller Park.

In this era of safe zones and overprotective parents, younger Americans are simply not seeing the worst human nature has to offer. Unlike previous generations, these young adults are largely sheltered from war, communist dictators, and existential hardship. Many younger Americans also seem to have personal identities forged by what the *New York Times* columnist David Brooks refers to as the "culture of selfism," meaning, "a culture that puts tremendous emphasis on self, self-care, and self-display." Rather than viewing morality as living up to some external standard like honesty, courage, and preserving liberty, Brooks writes, "Traditional morality has been replaced by self-indignation, being heard, telling your story and then, of course, condemning the bad people that make you feel judged or sad."[i]

To Generations Y and Z, the imagery of racist cops, open borders, and White privilege makes perfect sense. These younger adults do not seem to understand why former mansions in cities like Detroit are presently selling for under ten thousand dollars. Just as they don't seem to understand that the progressives who want to abolish entire police precincts today are the very same people who diminished the qualifications to become a police officer thirty years ago.

In recent times, the United States and other Western democracies have been significantly influenced by older Whites with little or no college education. While attending the university, it was always interesting being the only *older adult* in the classroom when the college professors would attempt the delicate task of reducing older Whites to unenlightened buffoons who watch Fox News every night. In that cat-and-mouse academic environment, I had to essentially defend "old and White" without *sounding* old and White. Unlike the professors, however, older Americans have seen the before and after of the progressive blueprint in a real-world setting. They have watched their children and grandchildren become part of the lost generation, where self-esteem was promoted without real accomplishment, traditional morality was ridiculed, gender roles were flipped upside down, and the thought of being patriotic to your country was akin to being a country bumpkin.

The results of this social experiment are becoming very apparent to those real-world Americans who live up close and personal with modern-day progressivism in the workplace, in the schools, and in their neighborhoods. They see a world quite different from the utopia being extolled in the lecture seats at the Ivy Leagues. Who is in the best position to witness the leftist experiment without bias? Is it the twenty-nine-year-old techie living in a *safe zone* neighborhood of Portland or Seattle? Or is it the working-class plumber who lives next door to a Section 8 public housing complex? These latter Americans have the common sense to understand unlimited immigration and open borders will eventually break the glue that has bound the American identity together for centuries. And they also understand life will never be fair—or free.

Many of these working-class voters certainly don't trust Republicans, but they didn't have a better option in 2016. So, they took a chance on the crazy guy for president because they were desperate. Are we living in a world in which the so-called elites were intellectually exposed by a segment of the US electorate that is the *least educated*? And if so, who are these millions of voters the Democrat elites are having such a hard time understanding?

Maybe it's the parents who worked their entire life for a college fund, only to see their daughter living back at home, angry, apathetic, and voting for Marxist politicians. Or maybe it's those middle-class Americans who work and live where the social engineering plays out in real time. This may be the construction worker who works side-by-side with an unqualified worker who was placed on the jobsite simply to meet a racial quota. Or it may be the factory worker who is the only one in the neighborhood who seems to go to work in the morning. Everyone else is on disability, collecting welfare, or living off their parents.

Trump's die-hard supporters are most likely to be Whites whose fathers and grandfathers fought in wars to protect liberty from tyranny, Latinos and Asians who escaped corrupt tyrants, and Blacks who understand the new master has some of the same qualities as the old master. These Americans know there is more to criminal behavior than disparate impact theory or racist cops. They understand giving able-bodied people easy money will keep them in front of their Xbox instead of finding a real job. This silent majority will listen to any politician who dares to speak up against the intellectual nonsense that has permeated nearly every corner of Western civilization. But these patriots also understand time is not on the side of putting God, country, and family ahead of wokeness, universal equality, and open borders.

There is an intellectual crisis occurring in Western civilization, and it may have been those with the least amount of education who exposed the folly. Any true intellectual should be worried when there is uniformity amongst one's peers. Today's monopoly of thought is not only arrogant, it represents the height of ignorance for any one person or group to think they have cornered the market on intelligence and knowledge. Just who can meet the scrutiny of having a real opinion without being labeled as racist, homophobic, or xenophobic?

Only they can.

The intellectuals of today have accomplished what the capitalist barons did during the Industrial Revolution. They have created their own monopoly in a day and age when society needs them to be free from dogma and unlimited in their ability to openly debate the great issues of our time.

The Democrats and Republicans *do* share something in common. Both have been inept at trying to implement their highest level of idealism. Conservatives haven't had a cohesive playbook since the 1980s. The establishment Republicans are the British redcoats of yesterday, standing in rigid formation and devoid of the know-how to fight back against a clever adversary. Their only hope now is that the strong personality of someone like Donald Trump can reverse the intellectual nonsense that has nearly split the US in two. The traditionalist should understand, however, that no individual will unite two worldviews that broke apart years ago. No single human being will be able to drain a swamp that has been polluted for decades with trillions of dollars and a revolving door between Wall Street and Washington, D.C.

Today's older Democrats are also starting to see how identity politics promote mass victimization, anger, and envy. Once the psychology of victimization is in place, there will be no bottom. The perpetual victim will seek endless ways to rationalize their personal shortcomings, and their corresponding anger can even turn full circle. The original friend can become the new foe. It won't be long before the revenge of the victim classes moves beyond Christopher Columbus and over to FDR and JFK. The radicalized leftist(s) will always want more than what was originally offered to them, and they will become hostile when their place in society is not in alignment with their expectations of grandeur.

What is true in raising kids is also true in how a society is managed. When a child's past is rooted in guilt and their future is steered toward envy and entitlement, they will become angry toward others and doubtful of themselves. They will follow false prophets who purport to have easy answers to complex life problems. This is what we have done to a generation of millennials whose lives have been forged by being "liked" on Facebook, harboring guilt about their heritage, and not having any reliable moral code aside from expressing feelings and being in harmony with the planet. We have allowed millions of individual psyches to become zombie-like, polluted by the politics of envy and robbed of the American spirit of taking big risks to accomplish great things.

By the end of my college journey, I knew the professors had found their winning hand. The Marxist academics have cleverly figured out how to embarrass and marginalize any voice that dares to speak out against the present-day assault on two-parent families, Judeo-Christian values, and limited government. It is true the college-educated radicals have been around since the 1960s. Today, however, their reach is found everywhere in society. The education establishment has become monopolized, religion is in decline, and the strong family structure from previous generations has become unglued. Ignoring these developments and hoping America will find itself again is not going to be remedied using conventional tactics. Throwing more money into urban areas to keep Blacks appeased is not going to work much longer. The original sin of slavery will no longer be reconciled with money and appeasement. Blacks now have enough money and representation to fight back against the dead White guys who still remain on the fifty and hundred-dollar bills.

I understand how talking this way has become very dangerous today; these kinds of conversations can trigger death threats, civil unrest, and maybe even a *societal divorce*. Predicting revolutions is like predicting earthquakes. They are inevitable, but there is no crystal ball that can predict timing and outcome. But just as the Covid-19 pandemic demonstrated how quickly life can change without warning, mass paradigm changes in the human order can be equally sudden and often cruel.

The goal today is to get ahead of our marital dysfunction before things grow even worse. The US *could* pursue a divorce arrangement that is initially amicable to both sides. For every Texan who wants to secede from the Union, there is a Californian who feels the same way. There is also a chance both parties will simply continue to live in the passive-aggressive public arrangement we exist in now. This type of societal compact is common in other countries, including our docile neighbor to the north. Contrary to public belief, Canada is not a large geographic swath of endless cooperation and harmony. Canada's population of thirty-five million people actually consists of three distinct worldviews, and they, too, have had their own aspirations of breaking up.[ii] Unlike Canada, the US plays a much larger role in the global community. If we continue to be an intellectually disconnected superpower that sends contradictory messages every time a new president is sworn in, the entire world order is at risk. Worse yet, the global community may simply conclude the US is no longer a reliable partner. Should this second course of action play out, it will likely mean the democratic traditions advanced by the US will see a dramatic decline. The global community will eventually favor a consistent China over a politically impotent and unpredictable America.

Not long ago, it seemed like we had it all, but over time, our marriage began to change. At first, we ignored the boorish behavior. We assumed our partner was going through a temporary hurdle or maybe a midlife crisis. Instead of throwing in the towel, we decided to stick it out. We turned a blind eye to the arrogance and abuse, hoping everything would return to normal. But in tolerating the anger, we compromised who we once were. We allowed ourselves to be dominated to the point of becoming irrelevant. We allowed ourselves to be placed inside a dark box.

If it hasn't already become apparent, one side of the marriage has grown inflexible, angry, and violent. If left unchecked, the anger will consume anyone who stands in its way. Yes, we also have our crazies. But the leftist crazies now control how mainstream Americans think, feel, and behave. If we don't stop them, they could soon be within reach of bringing the entire house down.

An American Divorce isn't about a bunch of crazy rednecks shooting AK-47s in the backwoods. Our plan is to unite like-minded White, Black, and Brown Americans with the most powerful set of ideas the world has ever known. Ultimately, this book is about regaining the confidence to return to who we once were. Our plan doesn't *have* to involve winning on every issue. In this sense, there is a chance a fresh and unfiltered

17

conversation could salvage the marriage. Just as there is also the chance a new conversation could lead to both sides agreeing to disagree and simply parting ways.

However, there is *also* the possibility that by talking on our terms, and not just theirs, they may become more violent than they already are today. Should this latter set of circumstances play out, we will consider putting them into the same dark place we are living in today.

Chapter 2: Why the Crazy Divorce Talk?

Apart from hydrogen, the most common thing in the world is stupidity.

—Harlan Ellison

The 1960s were a watershed moment in our marriage. In 1963, John F. Kennedy was assassinated, and to this day, we're not entirely certain how it happened. Shortly after JFK's tragic death, America became involved in a war that should have never occurred. Vietnam took the lives of nearly sixty thousand American soldiers and two million Vietnamese.[iii] In justifying the war, generals, congressmen, and presidents lied. In 1968, both Robert Kennedy and Martin Luther King Jr. were assassinated, and in 1972, a Republican president would resign over a Watergate scandal. After two hundred years of unbridled confidence and optimism, cracks began to emerge in the American psyche. The glaring imperfections of the 1960s political establishment opened the door to the agitators and the Marxists. The counterculture knew in their heart of hearts there had to be a better way than endless war, racial inequality, LBJ, and Nixon. Leftist agitators like Howard Zinn and Saul Alinsky found their opening in academia, and their influence has permeated throughout every segment of American society ever since.

Before we open the "divorce" conversation, let's begin with some basic clarification. Political labels are fluid and change throughout the context of time. At this moment, I'm not even sure what it means to be a "Republican" or a "conservative." Doesn't a fiscal *conservative* believe in balanced budgets? Isn't a social *conservative* supposed to believe in only two genders and one type of marriage? And wasn't the Republican Party once intended to represent both fiscal and social conservatives? If so, when did things begin to go sideways? What does it even mean to be a conservative or a Republican today?

And if we look closer at the Democrat side, what is the difference between a liberal, a progressive, or a Democratic Socialist? Is a Democratic Socialist a communist revolutionary who believes in free elections? Or is he/she a liberal who wants more socialism than capitalism? Is the present-day Democrat Party intended to represent the interests of workers over bosses, or have the "progressives" shifted to a globalist platform that seeks to put the US Congress on equal status with the United Nations?

Yes, both political parties are going through their own respective identity crises. Moving forward, I will use words like "traditionalist" or "our side" or "we" to distinguish those Americans who believe capitalism, democratic values, limited government, and strong families are the gold standard in finding the highest order in human affairs. A "traditionalist" is thus our protagonist, who, under the right set of mass-movement circumstances, would be willing to risk a *divorce* to help defeat the leftist "intelligentsia."

What do we mean by a "divorce" or a "mass movement"? Assuming the Democrats and Republicans are stuck in a dysfunctional marriage, what are the options when two groups of people can't seem to agree on anything?

20

They can essentially:

- Find common ground and remain in the marriage.
- Divorce their partner on good terms.
- Divorce their partner on bad terms.

Metaphorically speaking, our "divorce" goal *isn't* about helping Donald Trump and the Republicans. The "mass-movement" objective of the *traditionalist*, rather, is to assemble a widespread movement, which has the power to defeat an "ideological cancer" that has divided the US into a state of cultural and democratic paralysis.

The *cancer* in our marriage originated from those academics who have pitted millions of Americans against each other. If today's leftist elites and their enablers can be exposed and discredited, there exists the possibility the rest of us can begin to heal, unify, and find democratic normalcy. Moving forward, I refer to this outcome as *the* "good divorce."

The *second divorce* option is associated with a geographical breakup of the United States. Assuming there is no *good divorce*, what is the alternative? Is it possible the US could use a "Brexit-like" strategy where *red-* and *blue-*Americans simply agree to disagree, and then figure out a peaceful way to break the US into two separate countries?

The final divorce path(s) assume red- and blue-Americans remain stuck with no easy exit strategy for either side. From the perspective of the "traditionalist," this would imply a scenario where the leftists control the cultural norms, but *we* decide to *radically* challenge the power structure from inside the marriage. Applying this concept to revolutionary theory, today's conservatives would learn how to become tomorrow's radicals. In what would essentially become a zero-sum battle for control of the American identity, *we* would *agitate* the United States into a state of civil unrest and then hope to capitalize on the resulting chaos. Under this type of *mass-movement* scenario, the US military could play a significant role in the final divorce outcome.

Is it possible to walk away from our angry partner without conflict? Or is an American divorce destined to be *ugly* in outcome? These two questions should be thoroughly considered as we move through the questions of *why, who, and how?*

In trying to comprehend *why* the US is in such trouble, we need to begin by understanding what the *divorce fault lines* are really about. The long-standing dysfunction in Washington, D.C. goes much deeper than the talking points playing out on the twenty-four-hour news channels. Our underlying tensions are not rooted in race, taxation, abortion, foreign policy, or any other hot-button political issue(s). Ultimately, our problems go back to age-old question(s) that have plagued philosophers for thousands of years. Today's marital turbulence goes back to the fundamental philosophical question of *who* we are as people. Can human nature be perfected to guarantee future harmony to every person on the planet? Or do we live in a largely unknown reality where finding balance between benevolent and malevolent human impulses is the best way to advance the human condition?

Can life be free, fair, and *equal* in outcome? Or is the notion of universal equality an intellectual absurdity? Is widespread cooperation possible, or is *globalism* a misguided philosophical leap that could ultimately lead to the marginalization and potential destruction of the United States of America?

Are our *educated* kids and their college professors correct—are traditional-minded parents simply unenlightened stooges who "cling to their guns and their religion" because they don't know any better?[iv] Or are guns and a strong belief in a higher power prerequisites in protecting individual liberty? Until we realize where our marriage went wrong, it is silly to think there is going to be a game-changing breakthrough in Washington, D.C. once Donald Trump leaves office. Our marital troubles run deep, and they go far beyond Trump.

I'm not trying to win over the real *antagonist* with this book. I spent decades in their domain *as a minority*, and I understand what motivates them. Arrogance packaged as compassion, empathy, and "helping the greater good" rarely goes down without a real fight. The *devil* in our divorce story is not going to go away with mere words or self-help advice.[v] Nor is there going to be some future moment in time when millions of progressive elites conclude, "We were wrong; thank you for enlightening us." This isn't how human nature works. Yes, human beings can cooperate and love in the most trying of circumstances, but at the opposite end of our existence lies another reality rooted in power, self-centeredness, and dominance. By failing to acknowledge the full spectrum of who we are as living beings, the "educated left" have essentially placed our country in great peril.

Today, college students ask me, "Why is socialism bad? What is so wrong with the way the Norwegian countries are doing things?" Or they ask, "Why is communism flawed?" Before we answer these types of questions, let's listen to the sermon in greater detail:

Professor to class:

Religion, nation-states, and capitalism have reduced the human existence to a zero-sum battle for power and dominance. Millions of innocent human beings have died in the name of religious purity, ethnic cleansing, and the pillaging of resources. Once human beings are conditioned to cooperate on a global basis, the human reality will no longer be defined by endless competition, tribalism, and war. There will no longer be a need for armies, borders, or nation-states. Moreover, the reallocation of resources away from armies and guns could be used toward the collective good and proper stewardship of the planet. Once human beings are liberated by science and empiricism, humankind can finally become united by global cooperation and a set of shared values that transcend religion, nationality, and capitalism.

How does an everyday parent refute this professorial paradise with an adequate response? How do we flip our college-educated kids back to the idea that freedom from tyranny represents the highest level of utopia here on Earth? Unfortunately, the progressive worldview of human nature provides an easier path to inner peace and tranquility than the pessimistic alternative that comes with tolerating capitalism, guns, and inequality. And today, we no longer have the greater platform with our kids and grandchildren. The days of ministers, priests, and parents dictating cultural norms in America are long over. The radical professors from the 1960s have gone mainstream, and today, they control nearly every facet of our culture.

If given a choice, I'd much rather live in the world of the college professors over that of the twentieth-century preachers. Like the seventy-two virgins awaiting the Muslim martyr, there is a future paradise of peace, fairness, and equality for those willing to follow Bernie Sanders or Alexandria Ocasio-Cortez. But what happens to the West if universal peace and widespread harmony lie far beyond the reach of the human existence? What will the future hold to the United States if there is no such earthly reality as universalism and global harmony?

While attending college for those three decades, I saw utopia painted out in many ways. And make no mistake—once an idealistic student finds a way to intellectualize the notion that human beings can set aside egotism and selfishness, there is no turning back. If one buys into the intellectual narrative that human nature has yet another gear, it's easy to understand why the American founding (and the Jewish Zionist founders, for that matter) are so problematic to the left. If human beings are capable of mass cooperation and equal outcomes, the Founders failed miserably as human beings. They used coercive tactics to dominate and eradicate other cultures. And the villains weren't women; women were stuck at home with the kids. No, the true villains were men—specifically, White men.

The progressives, the liberals, the social Democrats, the Marxists—whatever name you want to assign today—are not only split with the Republicans over important political issues; both sides, in fact, have a much bigger problem. Every step forward for one represents an existential step backward to the other. Every new weapon system developed by Boeing or General Dynamics means a greater probability of peace to the traditionalist and a higher probability of massive death to the *do-gooder*. Every border wall that comes down represents global unification to the left and cultural fragmentation to the traditional right.

Facebook is another example that illustrates the philosophical debate of our time. To someone like Mark Zuckerberg, Facebook was the ultimate vehicle capable of steering humanity toward a greater level of understanding and global cooperation. To the human nature realist, however, it shouldn't have come as a big surprise that human beings with dubious intentions would also use social media platforms to spread hate, propaganda, and misinformation.

Make no mistake, it is difficult being on the pessimistic side of the human nature divide. Even when I had the facts on my side, I would still lose arguments to some professors. Here is another professorial diatribe that looked great on paper but not so great behind the scenes:

Professor to class:

Have any of you been following the debate about midnight basketball being rejected by the Republicans? I just can't understand Republicans. The legislators who oppose the idea of getting kids away from the drug dealers at night are the very same folks who will give tax breaks to the wealthy. Republicans will pay for more prisons, but they can't support a proactive program that attempts to keep at-risk kids off the streets at night.

When listening to the professor's argument at first glance, how could anyone oppose midnight basketball without being "mean-spirited" or "lacking empathy"? Granted, midnight basketball did seem great on paper. Instead of hanging out on the streets late at night, troubled kids could be playing organized basketball. But around that time, the largest city in my state was a cesspool of corrupt bureaucrats and "pay to play" politicians. As the midnight basketball idea was gaining traction with the local media, I had a politically connected customer ask my company to do an evaluation of several dilapidated buildings in the downtown district. Sure enough, the buildings were run-down and had been abandoned for years. When I reported the poor findings back to the customer, he told me the scoop:

"If that midnight basketball bill passes, I have an 'in' with the politicians. If I can buy these buildings for a nickel on the dollar, put a little money into some repairs, and build a handful of gymnasiums, I'll get a long-term lease and be clearing big money from the basketball."

Fortunately, for the taxpayers, the bill went down in the state legislature. Had it passed, however, here's what would have happened: my customer would have bought several old buildings in terrible shape and leased them back to the city for astronomical lease rates. Instead of a Bobby Knight running the program, it would have been Bobby, the-guy-who-knows-nothing-about-basketball, getting paid union wages to babysit a bunch of kids with poor adult supervision. And the politicians would have scored a *big* win-win. The program would have made for a great talking point during the next campaign. As to my prospective customer, he, his wife, and his kids would have sent out maximum campaign donations each year to keep the basketball leases in the family business for decades.

This story is a personal example of the bigger problem between the left and right. Even though I knew the midnight basketball scheme was a scam, I still couldn't beat the professor in this particular classroom debate. He sounded so empathetic, and I seemed so *cold* and *racist*. It's not that both sides don't see the same problems, they just see them in a completely different philosophical context. With today's Democrats, giving disadvantaged Americans welfare is compassionate and allows human beings to get back on their feet again. To us, giving people free stuff keeps them lazy and permanently dependent on government. With open-ended immigration, the right knows open borders will lead to balkanization and democratic tensions. To the progressives, all human beings are members of the same global community and should be assisted with free health care, education, and governmental aid. To them, the United States has unlimited resources to bring in millions of unskilled refugees in the name of helping humanity.

The list goes on and on. With the 2020 Covid-19 virus outbreak, it won't be long before both sides march to their respective corners in the human nature divide. The Democrats will probably say the virus shows the importance of cooperating beyond borders and nation-states, while the Republicans will conclude America should never again find itself in the position of relying on other countries like China for medical supplies. And the latter would be most right. To a human nature realist, the coronavirus pandemic has revealed the basic truth that in an existential crisis, human beings will take care of their own before they help others. What "intellectual" could be naïve enough to assume China will place Americans ahead of their own citizens? How could so many *smart people* in academia be so stupid about who we essentially are as living beings?

Beyond getting the human nature question wrong, the progressives also have a big problem with God. If human beings are perpetually flawed, who can be trusted to steer humanity to the utopia of universal outcomes and widespread harmony? With today's left, the UN, the psychologists, and the progressive intellectuals are the moral authority for humankind. Whereas the traditionalist distrusts all human beings with arbitrary power, the Democrat Socialist has intellectualized the notion there is a benevolent group of human *saints* who have discovered the master plan to unite seven billion people. But as the famed twentieth-century economist Milton Friedman once asked, "Just tell me where in the world you find these earthly angels who are going to organize society for us?" What human being can you trust over yourself, and perhaps a small number of friends and family, when all else fails?[vi]

- Dr. Anthony Fauci?
- Joe Biden?
- Barack Obama?
- Bernie Sanders?

- The UN Secretary-General?
- The Dalai Lama?

The traditionalist understands the answer to these rhetorical questions. If a person can count on one hand unconditional relationships based on friendship and love, he or she is very lucky. We don't elect superheroes to be public servants; we elect salesmen and sociopaths. Today, the talk is about Trump being a narcissist—as if Bill Clinton, Al Gore, and yes, Barack Obama, don't all fit the same psychological profile.

The Democrats are conflicted in ways that go well beyond politics. Unfortunately, the Republicans and libertarians also have their own philosophical problems. How smart were the conservatives in believing a balkanized Iraq was somehow suited for a democracy? How did George W. Bush and his neocon advisors come to the brilliant conclusion that a myriad of ancient tribal cultures were ready to embark on the democratic path of one person, one vote?

In this toxic red and blue relationship, we must admit we get the human nature issue wrong too. To the libertarian purist on the right, the market has more standing than God. When a pharmaceutical company invents a billion-dollar blockbuster, forget about having an FDA approve the final product. Human beings can simply trust CEOs will do the right thing. How stupid is this type of thinking? Didn't the United States already go down the path of unregulated capitalism in the last century?

Corporations will follow society to its lowest common denominator to maximize profits. Putting absolute faith in the marketplace is no different than what the Democrats are doing in over-trusting central planners and career bureaucrats. It almost feels as if both sides are spinning their wheels in the philosophical abyss with no logical endpoint in sight. As with most divorces, both sides share culpability in a marriage gone awry. Both voting blocs can easily point fingers at each other's flaws to reinforce their own misguided beliefs.

Until we fix our own underlying problems, how can we step beyond a broken marriage with confidence and conviction? How will we win over millions of mass-movement converts if we are just as confused as our partner is?

Today, the worst aspects of Republican-sponsored big business and left-wing academia have combined to define who we are as a civilization. While big business works to build an algorithm that can anticipate consumer spending habits to the penny, the academics have strong-armed millions of Americans into believing life can be *fair*. The present-day combination of mass consumerism on the right and pseudo-intellectualism on the left may just explain why the United States needs to consider the radical idea of blowing everything up and starting over.

Saul Alinsky (1909-1972) was the master 1960s agitator who wrote the script on how to take power away from the "Haves" of society. It is no longer a secret Alinsky's book, *Rules for Radicals*, captured the imaginations of a young Barack Obama and Hillary Rodham.[vii] Alinsky understood the hippie radical with long hair didn't represent the path of taking power away from the traditional *custodians* of society. Alinsky's script was essentially based on getting the hippie to the barber, buying him a nice suit, and then teaching him how to blend in with the people who would one day be overthrown. As Alinsky once opined:

> I feel confident that I could persuade a millionaire on Friday to subsidize a revolution on Saturday, out of which he would make a huge profit on Sunday, even though he was certain to be executed on Monday.[viii]

I think of this quote every time I see a mega millionaire hosting Democrat fundraisers at their mega beach houses. As Saul Alinsky alluded to, being rich and famous doesn't imply common sense. He knew once you learned someone else's rulebook, you could *club them over the head* into a state of submission. Alinsky understood no human institution could ever live up to its own set of standards. In this sense, he was certainly no twenty-first-century liberal in his realistic view of human nature. By learning how to exploit the inconsistencies and hypocrisy of those who are the moral and political protectors of society, Saul Alinsky recognized a clever societal instigator could use clandestine manipulation, tactics of humiliation, and self-doubt to eventually overthrow an entire societal establishment.

One may think words don't matter much, but Saul Alinsky taught us words can have more impact than guns and money. The 1960s radicals have figured out how to embarrass the traditional custodians of society, and they will shame any voice that dares to speak out against the present boundaries of political correctness. The academic elites have bypassed the First Amendment by stigmatizing much of the majority culture's normal thoughts and behaviors. The leftist fanatics have nearly won a stealth battle without having to fire a shot. There are now millions of Americans who can't speak their minds because they have been marginalized by intellectual thought barriers and societal shaming. Such tactics are not just happening at the University of Cal Berkley or Dartmouth. This type of one-sided intellectualism is occurring in the workplace, on TV, and in much of pop culture. Through the tactics of Saul Alinsky and others like him, today's traditionalist is sitting in a perpetual time-out chair. Worse, his critics have an open platform to disregard nearly every tradition associated with the belief America is an exceptional country.

If Alinsky was the field organizer of the left, Karl Marx (1818-1883) was the architect for today's Bernies and AOCs. Marx witnessed the harsh working conditions and wage

31

inequalities that arose during the initial stages of the Industrial Revolution in Great Britain.[ix] He concluded this type of workplace arrangement would open the doors to a future revolution between the workers and the capitalists. Marx wasn't an idiot. Even the most ardent defenders of capitalism should be able to admit in hindsight that anti-trust legislation and collective bargaining agreements from the last century were appropriate measures in finding a greater balance between workers and companies.

While Marx may have been correct with his initial diagnosis, he was inept in forecasting the future. Like today's Democrats and Republicans, Marx also got the human nature issue wrong. There was never a glorious revolution that freed the proletariats from the bourgeoisie in Western Europe or in America. With capitalism, the injustice is that a Mark Cuban can live a life of excess, while thousands of others are living on the streets. With Marxism, injustice occurs when one human being who aspires to do great things is held in the same societal standing as someone who is motivated to do nothing. When presented this choice, human beings will side with a wealthy Mark Cuban over a deadbeat brother-in-law who allows his wife to work two jobs while he plays video games all day. *By failing to realize the human existence is incompatible with universal equality, Marx's entire philosophical premise of a "workers' paradise" falls like a house of cards.*

Unfortunately for humanity, millions of people have died trying to capture Marx's elusive utopia. Even worse, his false prophecy of a classless world is making a dramatic comeback in the Unites States. To the social science professors, the fifty-million deaths in Russia and China had nothing to do with Marxism.[x] No, the deaths happened because "the people in charge didn't do things the right way." No economic system is perfect, but once the Marxists win over the masses, the storyline becomes very predictable:

- There is initial glee once the capitalist elites are strung up on poles.
- Shortly thereafter, economic shortages begin, private companies are nationalized, and inflation skyrockets.
- Political killings occur, and the elites flee the country.
- The strongman takes control under the guise of restoring social order.
- In the final chapter, there are no rich people left because everyone is poor—except for the dictator and his cronies.

I never understood how Karl Marx could be so wrong about his nineteenth-century, dire predictions yet be so in vogue with the artistic and intellectual minds of the last two centuries. Leftist diehards like Sean Penn and Michael Moore worship communist leaders in Latin American countries as if they are about to embark on a spiritual pilgrimage to the Holy Land. There is a ubiquitous, Marxist bias found at today's universities obsessed with race, class, and gender. In the never-ending battle to find social justice and equality, society is in a zero-sum battle against the privileged, White male and his patriarchal traditions. Today's intellectuals have convinced millions of Westerners to believe traditional values are outdated, capitalism is evil, and human nature is ready to advance to another level.

The great philosophers who most influenced Western civilization didn't fantasize about perfecting and equalizing the human condition. Men like Plato and Aristotle saw balance and virtue as a means to offset a man's inherent flaws. In fact, our entire model of Western civilization is based on the premise that man is born deeply flawed.

- Incentivizing man to love and to forgive may have been the most transformative moral development in mankind.
- Harnessing egotistical impulse toward the creation of wealth may have set the stage for the most profound economic transformation in human history.
- Placing sovereignty into the hands of individuals, rather than a king or dictator, was the biggest political advancement for mankind.

Christianity, Adam Smith, and the brilliance of the eighteenth-century philosophers explain the intellectual foundation of the United States. Yet, all three of these tenants are under constant intellectual duress.

- God is dead again.
- Capitalism is destroying the planet.
- America is flawed because of White, male privilege.

College students are being taught the problem with human beings does not lie in their own inherent self-centeredness, laziness, and envy. No, the root of the *human being* problem lies in the *institutions* that made man this way. It's not human nature that made us so nasty and selfish; it's religion and capitalism that have made us this way.

Our troubles are ultimately a debate about who we are as human beings as much as it is about our priorities as a country. No civilization can guarantee equality. Yet today, the so-called smart people want to guarantee equality at the expense of individual rights. With modern-day leftism, the "evil" is economic and social injustice, and the "good" is liberating the masses from racism, xenophobia, and capitalism. While reaching mass equality and saving the planet has become the new god, today's "devils" are CEOs, White men who show any type of traditional masculinity, stay-at-home moms, and evangelical Christians.

The true villains in our troubled marriage are those self-righteous intellectuals who have upended the legitimacy of any institution associated with the past. These academics and their minions in Hollywood are quietly tearing up traditional culture to pursue an intellectual utopia that will never exist. Using Alinsky-type tactics, the radicals of today are handpicking the warts of the past to sow constant guilt, agitation, and division onto our democracy. Some of the leftist agitators truly believe in a utopia of large-scale cooperation, borderless communities, and gender neutrality. Others will jump on the Marxist ride with Machiavellian intentions, knowing the fall of traditional Whites will bring satisfaction and opportunity to their own dubious ambitions.

Who are the true buffoons in this stealth battle for power and dominance? It is those Whites who have fallen prey to the guilt and propaganda that individual liberty was built on the cheap, and people with white skin are somehow guilty and privileged because of circumstances that happened in another era that is long since over. One must give the 1960s radicals their due. The academics stuck to their Marxist script with persistence and fervor, and today, they are within reach of overturning the most dominant power structure the world has ever known.

The ground zero in today's great twenty-first century divide begins at the universities and trickles down into every public school classroom. As a country, we allow future generations of Americans to be indoctrinated with such nonchalance, and then wonder how Bernie Sanders can attract millions of like-minded followers. While it's easy to blame the front-line teachers for what is happening, the real problem begins with us. We are no longer involved with what really goes on in the public schools, nor did we ever question the social engineers who created the subject matter being taught to our children. We trusted the system because it mostly worked in the last century. But today, the system is structurally broken beyond repair. Our schools have become indoctrination camps that prioritize globalism over Americanism, relativism over the Ten Commandments, and social justice over defending liberty.

Today, most American children will stumble with blank looks when asked, "Is America a great country?"[xi] And this is assuming they can find the United States on a map. Our kids are also depressed and anxious, and they are taking their own lives in an unprecedented fashion.[xii] Aren't human beings supposed to be happier in this era of modern psychology, do-gooder empathy, and global interconnectivity? Shouldn't our kids be smarter in this new world of technological advancement? It's now time to understand why the US system of education is the next battle line in our mass-movement discussion.

Chapter 3: Back to the Basics

A society with too few independent thinkers is vulnerable to control by opportunistic leaders. A society which wants to create and maintain a free and democratic social system must create responsible independence of thought amongst its young.

—*John Dewey*

The Founders understood a rigorous education was a prerequisite for maintaining democratic values. They knew a poorly informed voting populace would be ripe for manipulation, misrepresentation, and a likely return to autocratic rule. In this present-day era of easy voting-by-mail, rampant fake news, and low-performing public schools, one can easily argue this democratic apocalypse may already be underway in the United States of America.

In the early days of the country, education consisted of children from all ages being under the control of one teacher. As the US continued to grow, schools mirrored the Industrial Era "assembly line" that inspired business titans like Henry Ford. Students were grouped by age and grade, standard curriculums were made, and tests were used to measure progress. Arguably, the system worked well for what was essentially a homogeneous society that required more factory workers than engineers.

By the middle of the twentieth century, public education had become a federal behemoth, and politicians realized they could score political points by turning national news events into *helping the kids.* Each time there was a new fad in psychology or a momentary crisis in society, curriculums were changed to accommodate the social engineers and their friends in D.C. When "self-esteem" was the buzzword of the 1990s, for instance, the bureaucrats declared *promoting positive self-esteem* should be the most essential job of the educator. For the next two decades, teachers were mandated to embrace modern psychology to make the child feel "whole."

And who were the recipients of the self-esteem movement? You guessed it—the millennials. After years of undeserving praise and diminishing achievement, the experts began to change their tune about positive affirmation absent of real accomplishment. The elites realized an entire generation of Americans was prone to higher levels of "narcissism" and risk-averse behavior. Yes, the experts were wrong for decades, and today, millions of *adults* carry a level of self-importance that doesn't always match their contributions to society.

Can the millennials sue the psychologists and politicians for gross negligence? Can society go back in time and rewind millions of human minds? No, there will be no do-overs with the seventy million voters who were taught positive self-esteem is more important than possessing the character and courage to accomplish great things.

In 2000, the Republicans entered the scene of public education. George W. Bush upped the ante by creating a massive new program that promised "No Child Left Behind."[xiii] Billions of dollars later, the primary responsibility of the educator was to produce good test results. The test was the mechanism pushed by the Republican members in Congress to rationalize the massive federal dollars they had just piled onto the national debt—packaged as greater accountability in the classroom.

After Bush, Barack Obama came to the rescue with Race to the Top and Common Core.[xiv] Common Core is based on the bureaucratic notion every child in America has the same neurological hardwiring and level of parenting to learn at the same pace. I sympathize with today's public school teachers. Not only do they have to accommodate bureaucrats, disconnected parents, and disrespectful students, they must also play the game of using a one-size-fits-all boilerplate with every student in America.

As a former coach, I couldn't imagine adjusting my coaching style to satisfy a group of social engineers. A great crossover dribble, for instance, is a game changer for some basketball players. But not every player masters this skill, even after spending hours at home practicing drills. Conversely, I've had players who, after several practices, could *break an opponent's ankle* at half court with a *Hardaway-like* crossover. Using the logic of the central planners, I would be considered a bad basketball coach to those kids who couldn't master the crossover dribble. Yet I would be a *great* crossover coach if I inherited twelve kids with the ability to learn the skill with minimal instruction.

If the US was in a good place, teachers and doctors would share similar standing in society. But doctors don't belong to partisan unions that give millions of dollars to progressive politicians. Teachers can't have it both ways. The teaching profession can't be small, local, and nimble while being signatory members of a national union that is in near lockstep with the Democrats. At some point, teachers will have to look in the mirror and join our divorce discussion:

- Are most of today's teachers really educators?
- Or are many teachers merely pawns of the leftist fascists?

39

A true educator understands not only where a child is in life, but more importantly, where he or she can go to next. The left loves to talk about empathy, the importance of education, and, of course, *the children*. But where is the empathy in advancing a fifth-grade child, who never learned how to subtract and multiply, over to a sixth-grade algebra class? Can any of us adults imagine what it must feel like to be completely clueless in a classroom and then be teased into submission by dozens of other adolescent children? It sounds crazy, but this is what we are doing today with millions of young minds. The students are being run through the system like cars on an assembly line, and the adults wonder why so many of them are anxious, depressed, and hopeless.

Outside of a handful of students who can navigate the system, the United States is not inspiring its students to dream big and to love their country. The kids are instead placed into large buildings with hundreds of other immature minds and not enough adults with real moral authority. And rather than teaching its students how impactful the American founding was to all of humanity, our schools focus on the *bad* things the early settlers did to the slaves and the natives.

Forget the brutal atrocities the native tribes were doing to each other before the settlers arrived. Today, students are being taught the natives were all living together in universal peace and harmony until Christopher Columbus arrived. And forget the fact that, prior to the Civil War, every other civilization on Earth had practiced some form of slavery. Yet none of our forbearers went to war to end this abhorrent practice. How many students are being taught this important distinction? And how many of today's protesters realize over six hundred thousand Americans gave up their lives to end slavery?

America no longer educates its students with national pride, Judeo-Christian values, or rigorous academic inquiry. Whereas Chinese students are being taught to take pride in their communist and Confucian ancestry, American students are being taught to essentially hate who they are. What does Black History Month imply to a typical Black, Brown, or White student in third grade? It means people with white skin were very bad. Instead of teaching the Socratic method where every assumption of truth is treated with the utmost of academic scrutiny, today's students are instead indoctrinated with the politics of guilt, globalism, and privilege.

Our public schools represent the biggest civil rights injustice of our time. To a casual observer with even a basic level of common sense, putting three special-need students into a mainstream classroom represents an impossible set of circumstances for most teachers. How can any educator focus on academic excellence when they have thirty-five kids in a classroom, six of whom are very bright, three of whom have a learning disability, fifteen who are average learners, and eleven who have little to no parental support at home? This hypothetical example isn't a joke; it's a reality at nearly every public school in America. Just where do we find these superhero teachers who can obtain the best educational outcomes for dozens of students with completely different learning circumstances?

What are we doing to our kids with all these tests and the one-size-fits-all assembly line? If a child has artistic abilities, there should exist the option of smaller schools that are 50 percent art and 50 percent everything else. If a child has attention problems, there should be a school that can slow down its assembly line roll and make sure fractions have sunk in before algebra starts. If a child comes from an emotionally deficient family, forget about Common Core, multiple-choice tests, and academic proficiency altogether. Start with breakfast, lunch, basic life skills, and a learning environment that is safe, consistent, and emotionally in tune with the horrible set of at-home circumstances faced by thousands of American children.

Beyond the outdated public school assembly lines, today's elites are now peddling a package of "free college for all."

Should this *Santa Claus* proposition become an educational reality, the Democrats would enjoy a level of indoctrination in monopoly-like fashion. Think about this potential reality: what marketing agency wouldn't crave just a few hours of free, in-person exposure with its entire consumer base? Now imagine the college professors spending months and years with millions of young minds in an intimate classroom setting. Over 90 percent of college professors support Democrats.[xv] The progressives and the academics love to talk about diversity— unless, of course, the subject is intellectual diversity. Just what kind of education can one receive when nearly every professor has the same political outlook on life?

While at the university, I would sometimes question why there was so little intellectual "diversity" in the classroom.

Me:

I don't understand how an institution can call itself a university when students are only allowed to talk one way out of fear of being shamed or beat-up. I think safe zones are a joke in an academic setting. To me, your approval of what I can say or not say as a White male is no different than what McCarthy was doing in the 1950s.

Professor's response:

I welcome vigorous debate in my classroom. But are you denying the historical fact that White males have enjoyed levels of privilege, power, and influence at the expense of nearly every other person sitting here in the classroom?

After this type of exchange, I would immediately try to get a read on the classroom. Nearly every time, I observed a similar result. Some of the White male students were energized by my little diatribe, but I would lose most of the Black, Brown, and female classmates to the professor. The *disadvantaged* students seemed to accept the underlying logic that identity politics should take precedence over any other type of intellectual reasoning. Many of the students would become angry or dismissive of any sequence of logic that didn't begin and end with the intellectual premise that White males are simply too privileged to understand the full spectrum of a classroom debate. The genius of today's Marxist ideology is it pins the White-male antagonist into one corner of the room, while offering false hope and opportunity to the rest of the electorate.

In what is essentially another divide and conquer tactic used by today's social engineers, high school valedictorians are more likely to embrace "socialism" and "economic justice" over the previous underpinnings of limited government and individual sovereignty. In this brilliant reversal, the "smart" students are being taught to channel anger and hostility toward free markets and traditional values. "Free markets" and "traditional values" are, of course, the vehicles that foster *sexism, racism, corporate greed, destruction of the planet, and widespread discrimination.* The "white blood cells" that once protected the concept of "American exceptionalism" are now attacking their original host in unrelenting fashion.[xvi]

As a country, the United States, and its traditions, are getting mercilessly attacked from both the inside and outside. Students are being taught that many of the world's problems exist because of the United States and its imperialistic past. International students from visiting countries like China and Saudi Arabia are attending our universities, hearing firsthand from the *American* professors *how bad the United States is.* And the artists and celebrities are piling on by shouting out to the world the United States is a horrible country.

In previous centuries, Western elites understood the moral distinction between self-government and tyrannical government, socialism versus capitalism, and good versus evil. Just as previous intellectuals understood a vibrant democracy required its voters, in their totality, to be smarter than their elected elites. Today, illusionists use words like "empathy" to rationalize trillions of dollars in national debt. Or they use words like "tribalism" to denounce those who reject open borders and globalism. Millions follow along, putting complete faith in government, academia, and the media.

Should the US remain on its present path of "educating" the best and the brightest to "despise American individualism" while dumbing down the rest of the electorate in dysfunctional public schools, we won't need a crystal ball to predict what will happen next. The United States will remain on a path defined by two radically different *red* and *blue* Americas. One side of the marriage will be younger, Browner, and Blacker, while the other side will be older and Whiter. The former will likely follow the elites on a leftward march toward nanny-state governance, open borders, universal outcomes, and the politics of guilt, envy, and empathy. The latter will clamor for a fleeting past that is quickly moving beyond the horizon.

The "cancer" or "devil" in our marriage originated in academia and has since spread throughout every classroom in America. One would think students would be smarter in an era where tablets have replaced pencils and paper. Yet today, a student can graduate from college and not understand the most basic truths of the human existence. How can a democracy sustain itself when its most educated people are too ignorant to understand the promise of equality for all will ultimately lead to tyranny by a few?

Nowhere is the failure of the educational establishment more profound than in cities like Memphis, Milwaukee, and Detroit. In some majority-Black school districts, there exist schools where less than ten percent of the students are proficient in any one subject.[xvii] Assuming a democracy requires an educated citizenry, what is the answer in cities that have more homicides in a week than some countries have in a decade? Are White people to blame for poor-performing inner-city schools, incredible levels of urban violence, and racial tensions? Or do Blacks have to step up and fix their own problems?

We are officially moving into the dangerous waters of race in America. In today's academic climate of relativeness, it is considered insensitive to talk negatively about other cultures. To the sympathetic Whites marching in the Black Lives Matter protests, inner-city dysfunction is to be blamed on systematic racism. It is not the Blacks who should be blamed for their actions, but rather the Whites.

Our next step is to move the discussion over to a larger audience. Who are the various players in a bad marriage gone awry? What do we mean when we say "Whites," "Blacks," and "Browns"? What do these subgroups think of when they hear words like: mass movement and divorce?

We will begin answering this question by shifting our discussion to the *big elephant* in America's living room. A bloody civil war couldn't right the big wrong of slavery. Trillions of dollars in governmental spending haven't overcome the "original sin." And the leftist agitators will continue to project the Black/White divide onto "racist holdouts" until time runs out.

Barack Obama likes to say, "It's time to have a real conversation about race in America."[xviii] But what's real to Obama may be much different than what's real to many other Americans. It's now time to begin a real conversation about the legacies of slavery and what they mean to a marriage in great peril.

Chapter 4: The Original Sin

I have more respect for a man who lets me know where he stands, even if he's wrong, than the one who comes up like an angel and is nothing but a devil.

—Malcolm X

In 2018, the *Black* Republican nominee for the US Senate in Michigan, John James, garnered less than five percent of the Black vote in Detroit.[xix] James was a combat pilot and successful businessman, but was rejected in the same manner Trump was in 2016. John James was simply *too White* to win in Detroit. Outside of the fringes, the real twenty-first-century battle with race has little to do with skin color. Today's racial battle is ultimately about culture, politics, and *power*. Blacks can call out Whites because Whites are *privileged,* but Whites can't critique Blacks because the former are *disadvantaged.* This dynamic has scared the daylights out of not only most Whites, but also every public relations department in corporate America.

The antagonist in this book has a mostly white face. As with most divorces, there are others standing on the peripheral looking to take advantage of a divided marriage. I spent a lot of time up close and personal in inner-city schools and housing projects. As we shall soon discuss, there is more to the Black/White story than racist cops and discrimination in the workplace. I'm not looking to pick unnecessary fights in this book, but there is no denying the symbiotic relationship between the Black voter and the White fascist. Today, this quid pro quo alliance is stifling free speech and wreaking political havoc on our great country. Who would dare say anything bad about Black culture and not expect to be demonized as a racist? And who can take any pride in the founding of America without being privileged?

We have learned from Saul Alinsky that words can shape a powerful narrative. Today, it is a "no-no" for Whites to negatively critique other cultures, unless of course, they condemn their own culture. The do-gooders have created an entire nomenclature that incentivizes "good" thoughts while punishing "bad" thoughts. Words like racism, inclusion, and diversity have the power to shape every aspect of our lives. If one does not fully embrace the idea of *inclusion*, being packaged to the masses as *diversity*, they are quickly tarred and feathered a *racist*.

As an American, I feel tremendous pride in knowing a handful of settlers were willing to risk everything to guarantee our freedoms today. Men like Franklin and Washington didn't *have* to do what they did in the late 1700s. By taking the American side in the Revolutionary War, Benjamin Franklin split his family in two.[xx] Thousands of others died to pursue the risky proposition that human beings should be able to control their own destiny. Contrary to the sermons given at most universities, the *original sin* in America's founding had nothing to do with who could vote and who couldn't vote in 1787. Granting White males with property the right to vote was a radical departure from thousands of years of tyrants, kings, and despots with nearly unlimited power. Any twenty-first-century academic who is unwilling to acknowledge the historical significance of diminishing the arbitrary power of a king or a pope is a modern-day fool.

The true original sin of the founders was not reconciling slavery to Thomas Jefferson's notion: "All men are created equal." By allowing this distinction, Blacks were essentially *dehumanized* into property instead of being recognized as human beings.

Even though the Founding Fathers had game-changing ideas for humanity, I suspect many of them knew this monumental contradiction would come back to haunt the Republic for the ages. But they also understood the Southern delegates would never ratify the US Constitution if slavery was on the table. So, they kicked the can down the road. I understand Blacks have paid the biggest price in the greatest contradiction of our nation's history. But thousands of Whites paid the ultimate price during the Civil War. And here we are today—still trying to sort out a two-hundred-fifty-year-old mess.

In the entire realm of life, we are all God's children. All of us are small, replaceable, and mortal. But in the realm of how to live the most ideal life, we have choices as human beings. And those choices matter in a democracy. After spending years personally working in Black-majority housing complexes, I was shocked by the emotional, intellectual, and physical neglect so easily dismissed as normal parenting. The enabling Whites will predictably say bad parenting is found in every race. But I am confident these *social justice warriors* are not living in the same world many of our police officers call "work." If today's empathetic Whites were actually living in the neighborhoods they claim to care so much about, there would probably be as much—if not more—anger directed at those bureaucrats who have spent decades defining compassion as placing millions of voters into a permanent cycle of dysfunction and dependency.

For years, I witnessed everyday dysfunction from mostly Black households that went beyond comprehension. Just as I witnessed poor-performing K-12 schools that would never be tolerated anywhere else in America. If you don't believe my observations, pay closer attention to the first ten minutes of the morning news. Go spend a week in an urban motel located just outside the downtown entertainment district in nearly any large American city. Or simply look at the statistics.

Before the Great Society programs of the 1960s, 60 percent of Black parents were married.[xxi] Using recent data, *81* percent of Black children in cities like Detroit are born out of wedlock.[xxii] In some inner-city high schools, there exist entire graduating classes where not a single student is prepared to move onto college.[xxiii] Sure, there are some young men and women who can find personal success without a solid foundation of parenting and schooling, but these impressive human beings are outliers. Single-parent families are undeniably the biggest predictor of unwanted pregnancies, low wages, or imprisonment.[xxiv]

Even though Blacks make up only 13 percent of the US population, 41.6 percent of welfare recipients are Black.[xxv] In terms of prison incarceration, 34 percent of all inmates are Black.[xxvi] Between 1980 and 2008, Blacks committed more than 50 percent of all homicides in the US.[xxvii] And although this next statistic will never show up on the nightly news, *89 percent of all black murder victims are killed by other Blacks!*[xxviii] In cities like Chicago, *dozens* of Blacks are shot by each other every weekend. And some of the victims are innocent children. Where is the outrage when two or three children are caught in the crossfire of a weekend shooting spree? *Why does it seem like Black lives only matter when the perpetrator is White?*

These are tough statistics for the White apologists to refute. How do the millennial protesters and their baby-boomer professors place so much blame onto *racist cops* when it is Blacks killing other Blacks in such an alarming fashion? And at what point will the media begin telling *the other side of the story* of what it means to be Black in America?

My goal here isn't about protecting "bad apples" in law enforcement. There are many cops who have no business wearing a badge. But those "woke" protesters who typecast every police officer from afar have no idea what these men and women go through in cities like Houston, New York City, and Los Angeles on an everyday basis.

In the aftermath of the 2020 police killings, corporations are stepping over themselves to change their hiring policies. Today, companies are doling out billions of dollars to advance the causes of social justice and diversity. But where do these corporations think they are going to find a stream of Black talent in communities with 70-80 percent out of wedlock rates? One doesn't have to have a PhD to understand the reality that early childhood dynamics significantly influence a human being's ability to process cause and effect, language, attitude, and ethics. In what has essentially become a chicken-versus-the-egg question, are today's Blacks underrepresented in important levels of society because of systematic racism, or is their reduced standing better explained by a preponderance of unstable families and dysfunctional public schools?

Much of the Black identity is measured by other Blacks in how they interact with Whites. The power of Uncle Tom is alive and well. This nineteenth-century literary caricature continues to prevent many Blacks from embracing few aspects of White culture.[xxix] Today, Uncle Tom is the mechanism that groups independent thinkers like Ben Carson and Clarence Thomas into the lexicon of house Negroes and sellouts. Any Black who finds personal success through the back channels of White culture understands the risks of being too aligned with the *master*. Sadly, the small percentage of Blacks who find cultural, emotional, and political alignment with traditional Whites must watch their backs from every angle. These Americans still encounter pockets of ignorant Whites while also being shunned by much of their own race.

The perfect role model for Blacks *should* have been President Barack Obama. Unfortunately, Obama put politics and his agitating instincts ahead of having real discussions about race in America. Obama danced around the core issues of greater individual accountability, responsible parenting, and escaping the life-long dependency that seems to follow federal dollars and public housing complexes.

Before the Covid-19 pandemic, Trump had Blacks working in greater numbers than ever before,[xxx] but he may still only receive less than 10 percent of their vote in 2020. I hope I'm wrong with this prediction. Should more Blacks move away from the do-gooder Whites at the voting booth, our problems could become much less complicated. If more Blacks were willing to spread their votes, hearts, and minds beyond a Democrat ideology that fosters permanent reliance to the state, traditional Whites and Browns would have greater empathy in helping Blacks with bad cops, workplace hiring, and shutting down terrible schools. If Blacks didn't have so many conflicts in finding self-reliance, more Whites and Browns would open *their* hearts to better understand the different reality that comes with being Black in America. And if Blacks dealt with killer cops without looting and burning down buildings, they could expand grave instances of police injustice into a lasting movement that transcends skin color and political affiliation.

Unfortunately, the inherent contradiction of slavery with the Declaration of Independence is a structural fault line that has been manipulated by bad actors from every race. If a societal divorce were as easy as an individual breakup, Blacks and Whites would have parted ways centuries ago. Since the messy aftermath of slavery and the horrendous Civil War, the US has taken awkward and ugly paths to correct its original sin. There was the view slavery was morally wrong, but society had to do everything possible to shield the White culture from a dysfunctional slave culture. This plan was accomplished with "three-fifths votes," "separate but equal," and "Jim Crow."

Under these societal arrangements, many Whites were Christians by day, and broad-based haters by night.

In the 1960s—and a hundred years removed from the Civil War—the Democrats upped the ante on assimilating Blacks and Whites. Facing the political reality of 90 percent of the Black population being loyal to Lincoln's Republican Party, Lyndon Johnson dreamed of a "Great Society" that would eradicate poverty and get more Blacks into the mainstream of society. Rather than solving the Black/White divide through an aggressive cultural and racial showdown, the elite Whites decided to get Blacks into the game gradually, and they did so primarily through affirmative action initiatives, HUD housing placement, extending welfare policies, and pressuring their labor friends to open the doors of the union halls to more Blacks.

Fifty years later, the level of poverty for Blacks remains largely unchanged.[xxxi] After trillions of dollars, an overwhelming majority of Blacks are still sitting on the backbenches of American society.

As a former federal contractor, I personally witnessed how quotas end up playing out in the real world. Black community activists in cities like Detroit and Cleveland were always uneasy when a crew of Whites, *and Latinos*, would show up to perform construction work without majority-Black representation. Contracts were thus mandated to demonstrate at least 50 percent of the workforce was Black. Companies that failed to validate their "participation rates" through certified payroll were forced to pay fines and penalties.

What was the most common result of the social engineers? Most companies would factor the fines and penalties right into their overall bids. Companies knew how difficult it was to pull highly skilled workers off the street. Throw in the added employment requirements of passing a drug test and having a valid driver's license and it was nearly impossible to meet the quota guidelines. The cities that needed the money the most often wasted millions of dollars trying to promote *diversity*.

While there will be outliers who can overcome tremendous odds, society will never be able to buy the emotional stability and self-independence rooted in unconditional love and parental boundaries. The academics will, of course, continue to intellectualize and project Black dysfunction back onto Republicans, racist CEOs, and privileged Whites. And the apologetic Whites will line up en masse to show the world how empathetic they are.

To the social engineers, more money and greater tolerance are the keys to finally finding social justice and economic equality for Blacks. Today, the Democrats want to double down on the failures of the 1960s Great Society with a new trillion-dollar behemoth called the *Green New Deal.*[xxxii] To put some perspective on this legislative initiative, groups like the American Action Forum have forecasted this proposed bill would cost anywhere from fifty-one to ninety-three trillion dollars, or six hundred thousand dollars per US household.[xxxiii]

The Whites who want to keep throwing money at the problem of race don't see, or simply refuse to see, the everyday dysfunction of a culture that desperately needs to try a different approach than spending trillions of dollars. There is also a profound disconnect occurring between the *empathetic Whites* from afar and those *real-world Whites* who witness the double standards in their everyday lives. Unfortunately, this divergence leads us to another unpleasant question with race: When does simply being "*aware*" cross the line of being a "*racist*"?

Should human beings ignore the reality that walking around the wrong areas of most American cities is a bad idea, or should they keep their eyes wide open and hope everything will work out okay? Am I racist in thinking 80 percent out-of-wedlock birth rates and poor-performing schools will keep most Blacks at the bottom rungs of society well into this century? Am I racist for saying it is time for Blacks to finally get their act together with greater accountability?

Just how long was the affirmative action plan supposed to last? Fifty years? A hundred years? And what were the benchmarks to measure progress? We know the answer to these questions: there were *never* any timetables or benchmarks. Today's Whites must keep paying an eighteenth-century tab that has no endpoint in sight.

In 1961, Martin Luther King Jr. said the following:

> Do you know that Negroes are 10 percent of the population in Saint Louis and are responsible for 58 percent of its crimes? We've got to face that. And we've got to do something about our moral standards... We know that there are many things wrong in the White world, but there are many things wrong in the Black world, too. We can't keep on blaming the White man. There are things we must do for ourselves.[xxxiv]

This statement was made nearly sixty years ago. Why is there still so much dysfunction found in Black culture? Just how long do Whites have to stay in the penalty box for sins last committed 150 years ago? And when will enough Blacks be able to embrace self-government without the help of Whites?

I understand prejudice and discrimination are real—I'm not living in some kind of fantasy world where everything is perfect with White people. I have no doubt law-abiding Blacks carry a level of irrelevance most Whites simply can't understand. The Black twentieth century writer Ralph Ellison spoke of feeling "invisible" in a White-dominated world: "*I am invisible, understand, simply because people refuse to see me.*"[xxxv] Few Whites can sympathize with the everyday reality that comes with being marginalized to the point of feeling *irrelevant* as a human being. And most Whites can't comprehend the feeling that comes with being under constant suspicion. Imagine living in an everyday reality where a police officer is not viewed as a friendly protector, but rather a potential tyrant who has a license to kill.

Imagine walking into a bank, or any other place of business, and dealing with the unnecessary stares and the added suspicion. Envision walking into a job interview, knowing the person conducting the interview has no intention of ever hiring a Black person. And imagine being a parent, knowing your child is going to face a reality no other child in America will ever have to consider. How does a Black parent tell their child the United States is so great when America's most glaring imperfection is always in plain sight?

As with most bad marriages, Blacks and Whites have plenty of evidence to justify their ill feelings toward each other. Both groups continue walking on eggshells hoping one racially charged police encounter doesn't escalate into widespread civil unrest.

In my final years at the university, I was troubled by a trend that has since moved outside of the classroom. In the late 2000s, it was becoming commonplace for the professors to denounce White culture in an open forum. If this level of hatred was directed at any other demographic beyond Whites, professors would be fired, and universities would be in full damage-control mode. But just as Blacks understand the double standards that come with a job interview or an encounter with the police, traditional Whites understand the double standards that come with what to say or, more importantly, what *not* to say.

Blacks are attending college today in greater numbers.[xxxvi] The social science agitators are fanning Marxist tensions between Blacks and Whites because they view twenty-first-century Blacks as potential foot soldiers in that long-awaited revolution against the millionaires and billionaires. In an era when celebrities and athletes have a bigger platform than nearly anyone else in society, the social justice warriors at the universities have figured out that a Black athlete or entertainer who makes it big may become the perfect spokesperson to carry the Marxist fight into the living rooms of every American household.

Should my anecdotal observations from the classroom be correct, educated Blacks will become even more emboldened to aggressively reject the *evil* ways of White America. Today, the term for such an awakening is referred to as "woke," and leftist movements like Black Lives Matter and Antifa have a much different motivation than what MLK Jr. preached in the 1960s. This potential set of circumstances, if not dealt with in an honest conversation today, could become the match that lights the divorce fuse of tomorrow.

We know the White apologists are very effective at using powerful slogans during Black History Month, but the great twenty-first-century myth is that White Democrat politicians have the best interests of Black Americans at hand. Do the Democrats *really* care more about Black children, or do they care more about powerful teacher unions? Do the Democrats *really* want more Blacks to be self-reliant, or do they want Blacks to remain a loyal voting bloc? What the leftist elites truly want is to maximize their political power against traditional Whites. And the best way to accomplish this goal is to never let Black voters forget the sins of the past.

The White college students who feel so much pain and guilt at the Black Lives Matters protests don't seem to understand their "empathy and guilt" will only make the problem of race worse. Rather than focusing on stronger family structures, better schools, and having new discussions, the increased protests and lawlessness will only motivate both sides to distrust each other even more.

Just as Blacks have a reason to be angry about slavery, Whites have the right to say, "At what point can we move on from a 150 years ago?" Just as Blacks have a right to want more, Whites have the right to say, "No more." And just as the empathetic Whites have the right to suggest more money and time is needed, all Americans have the right to say, "We're done being African Americans or Latino Americans; we want to be judged only as *Americans*."

Martin Luther King Jr. also famously said:

I have a dream that my four little children will one day live in a nation where they will not be judged by the color of their skin, but by the content of their character.[xxxvii]

A colorblind America will never occur if the US remains on its current path of guilt, fear, and identity politics. Nor is there going to be a near-term reconciliation between Blacks and Whites under the precondition that Whites are *too privileged* to take part in a real discussion on race. A colorblind society will be found when enough Whites, Blacks, and Browns look at each other for the first time and say, "Friend, we're in this together as Americans. Judge me by who I am as an individual, and let's put our country back together."

I recognize Blacks were invited to the original party with chains and shackles. But how much longer can this unfortunate past be leveraged before both sides simply give up on trying to understand one another? How long will it take before more Blacks realize their biggest obstacle in America is not from those Whites who seem indifferent, but rather from those Whites who *seem to care so much*? And how much longer can today's Marxist social science professors be allowed to fan the flames of race before the US breaks up into two countries?

When can the United States begin a real conversation on race? When can we discard divisive words like Black, Brown, and White altogether? Why can't we all have real debates in the country that authored First Amendment rights? And most profoundly, when can the Americans of today accomplish what the Founding Fathers couldn't do and what MLK Jr. hoped to do—that is, create a *new way* where individual character and merit become more important than skin color?

Beyond the Black and White divide, there are approximately eighty-five million *Brown* Americans trying to sort out the tension and acrimony.[xxxviii] Today, we use words like Hispanic, Asian American, and Pacific Islander with such ease and arrogance, as if someone of Mexican descent shares the same cultural values as someone of Dominican descent, or if someone of Chinese descent is somehow close in perspective to someone who is Japanese. This method of identity politics is not only absurd, it undermines the most fundamental American creed of E Pluribus Unum: (*Out of many, one.*)

What do Asian and Latino Americans think about all this crazy *marriage* and *divorce* talk? Is the US a standard-bearer of individual freedom, or is American idealism simply a ruse only intended to benefit White males? Do older Whites hate foreign people who don't have white skin, or have the Democrats been successful in typecasting traditional Americans as mean-spirited and xenophobic?

I am convinced there will not be a successful mass-movement result without a cultural and political alignment between traditional-minded Whites and Latino and Asian Americans. President Trump should have understood this by now. It is now time to move beyond Trump, the Democrats, and the Republicans; it's time to begin a new and much needed discussion between Browns and Whites without any middlemen standing in the background.

Chapter 5: The Twenty-First-Century Swing Vote

The land belongs to people who work it with their own hands.

—Emiliano Zapata

My father was an example of the classic, twentieth-century immigrant story. He came to the US at the age of seventeen with ten dollars. He spoke zero English and spent his first years as a vagabond living in cheap motels and old trolley cars. Eventually, he would learn English, marry, have children, and start his own business. Later in life, I came to realize my father's biggest sense of accomplishment wasn't about making money or starting a company. His biggest source of pride, beyond family, came from knowing he had what it took to be an American.

We should be able to understand the twenty-first-century progressive mindset now. Today's do-gooders would explain with resounding conviction and empathy, how unfair it was that my dad had to sleep in abandoned railroad cars while some billionaire was living it up in Monte Carlo. Whereas the traditionalist views the primary struggle in life as one against his own primitive ego, the progressive views struggle in the Marxist context of inequality and injustice. While my dad was

59

sleeping in cheap motels in 1957, billionaires like Howard Hughes were sleeping with beautiful women in luxury Vegas penthouses. Using the logic of today's left, my dad should have first visited the Department of Social Services for an impressive array of governmental benefits before he got angry at Howard Hughes for having so much money.

One doesn't have to be a Sigmund Freud to understand the negative energy associated with obsessing over the success of others. While society must be mindful when power and wealth are limited to only a handful of people, how did today's *intellectuals* arrive at the philosophical assumption that economic equality is more important than the ability to pursue happiness without having to worry about the watchful eyes of politburos and cartels?

I'm glad my dad didn't obsess over Howard Hughes's massive wealth differential. Like many rich people, Hughes wasn't all that happy. It takes a lot of energy to protect a vast fortune from predators and insincere friends. In 1976, the reclusive Hughes would die on a flight to Texas after a tragic battle with mental illness, loneliness, and malnutrition.[xxxix] Meanwhile, my mother and father had just bought a house with enough land to start a family business. My immigrant parents entered the US from the very bottom and ended up living the American dream.

I live in a diverse metropolitan area and have friendships and business relationships with people from many different cultures. As a businessman and citizen, I don't care where someone was born. I just want to see newcomers contribute and have emotional buy-in with their new country. I don't know what the math is for bringing in either too many new people or not enough, but I support opening the doors to as many smart and hardworking people as possible.

We know why today's Democrats want to open the floodgates to "Brown" immigrants—they want the votes. The real prize lies in putting Texas into a perpetual "blue" column.

This reversal would mean the end of traditional Whites having any further influence in American politics. The coastal Democrats would finally escape the inconvenience of having to patronize the White working-class stiffs in the Rust Belt states.

Who are the approximately 85 million Americans that originated primarily from Latin America and Asia? Breaking this number down, 60 million Browns are Latinos, 20 million are Pacific Rim Asians, and 3.5 million are Muslims.[xl] Let's take a closer look at the numbers and voting patterns of Browns, Blacks, and Whites in the 2016 presidential election:

2016 Presidential Vote Breakdown[xli xlii]

1. Brown (Latino): 66% for Clinton, 28% for Trump

2. Brown (Pacific Rim Asian): 65% for Clinton, 29% for Trump

3. Brown (Muslim): 77% for Clinton, 11% for Trump

4. Black: 89% for Clinton, 8% for Trump

5. White: 57% for Trump, 37% for Clinton

We will begin our *Brown* discussion with the approximately sixty million Latino Americans in the US.[xliii] Latinos will continue to grow in population due to higher birth rates and open-ended immigration policies. As they increase in population, and in votes, the push will be on by both political parties to expand their appeal to this culturally diverse group of Americans. Should the Democrats win this battle, and the Latinos end up becoming the same predictable voting bloc as the Blacks, the GOP would find themselves in the same irrelevant status as they are in California today. Under this reshuffling of the Electoral College cards, the national

Republicans would become dinosaurs stuck in a political no-man's land.

I have worked side by side with Mexican men whom I trust and respect at a family level. There should be little question that Latinos will perform the manual labor most Whites and Blacks will avoid—even when the latter are offered higher wages. And contrary to President Trump's rhetoric, most foreign-born Latinos are lawful human beings who simply desire a better life.

It is true not all Latinos are like the men I crossed paths with inside the construction industry. There is no denying Mexico has big problems with gang violence and corruption; the cartels are omnipresent in many areas of Latin America. Mexico is ranked as one of the most dangerous countries in the world.[xliv] Should the United States continue to turn a blind eye to border security, the level of violence and corruption found in Mexican cities like Tijuana and Juárez will find its way to US cities like Miami and Phoenix. Americans who visit Mexico, Brazil, or Columbia understand the power of cash and selective law enforcement. Turning a blind eye to corruption will kill any democracy, and tolerating corruption is the kryptonite that seems to follow the Latinos from every country.

The Latino people are not fools—they know their homelands are being overrun by the cartels and corrupt politicians. These Americans will support an aggressive US president who can properly distinguish between *the good and the bad* that countries like Mexico have to offer.[xlv] Trump didn't have to humiliate an entire Latino-American population to win over more working-class Whites. This strategy was shortsighted and *wrong*. Latinos would have supported Donald Trump in greater numbers had his rhetoric been sophisticated enough to distinguish the *murderers and the rapists* from the millions of Latinos who are hardworking, socially conservative, and *good* human beings.[xlvi]

I am hoping that today's undecided Latinos look past Trump's rhetoric and understand the significant seat they hold at the table. If one is a Latino watching the White politicians banter back and forth, which group of Whites is most likely to lead America on the strongest path forward? Is it those progressive Whites who believe girls are not really girls and boys are not really boys, or is it those traditional Whites who believe strong female and male identities are essential to parenting and protecting the future of their country? Is it the Marxist path of Bernie Sanders and Alexandria Ocasio-Cortez or the freedom path of George Washington and Abraham Lincoln? Do Latinos want to follow dependent Blacks and socialist Whites, or do they want to follow those Americans who believe in strong families, limited government, and protecting liberty from tyranny?

I acknowledge some right-wing Whites despise foreigners, but these haters are a small group in a very large population. Traditional Whites are *not* xenophobic. What the traditionalist dislikes are unenforced laws, open borders, and federal immigration policies that don't consider a person's character, intentions, and skill sets. What traditional voters desire from other cultures, and countries, are productive and law-abiding human beings who will never allow cartels, autocrats, and tyrants to have more power than an individual sovereign. How many people would invite a guest into their house who has a criminal record? What previous civilization was able to remain cohesive and strong without enforcing its own laws, borders, and dominant cultural traits?

Traditional Whites need to start asking themselves some difficult questions as well. There will not be a peaceful cross-border transfer of twelve million law-abiding Mexicans back to Mexico.[xlvii] Nor is it in the best interest of our country to do so.

In what would represent a first mass-movement step, the traditionalist should begin the process of creating an effective immigration platform both sides can easily understand. Of course, there needs to be legal and regulated immigration. It would not be difficult to verify who is in the country illegally. A functional immigration policy would give "illegals" a grace period to report their standing in the US. Companies would be granted a similar period to E-Verify their workers. Those individuals who can demonstrate and document—via their employment records—a positive contribution to society, would be granted temporary visas from their countries of origin. Any "illegal immigrants" with a gang affiliation and/or criminal record would be deported. And those who didn't voluntarily come forward would be deported once they have any encounter with law enforcement or any other governmental agency.

Allowing sanctuary cities and turning a blind eye to undocumented immigrants would be enforced as illegal acts on a federal basis. Eventual citizenship would require the ability to speak and write English and a proven track record of positive citizenry. In terms of building walls, the cost and the ability of deterring people from going over, around, or below any such barrier would have to be measured with results and not political rhetoric.

As we consider how to repair a very broken country with new alliances, the goal of the traditionalist would be to aggressively dispel the propaganda that "traditional Whites hate Latinos." In what may come as a surprise to the progressive elites, much of the working-class Latino population is not ready to jump into the same political relationship the Democrats have with Blacks. In many cases, Latinos carry a level of hostility against Blacks that is rarely discussed at liberal think tanks. When I would mention this cultural friction to the college professors, this would be a common *academic* response:

Professor to class:

Well, that is understandable. Hispanics, like African Americans, are competing for the crumbs in a capitalistic system that favors Whites. This economic diversion results in primitive conflict and tribal behavior between the various Have-Not subgroups in American society.

I witnessed a different reality on the ground, however. Once our Latino employees saved twenty thousand dollars, they were out of the city and into the suburbs. These men and their families were in a race against time to get their kids away from the dysfunction associated with much of urban Black culture. Like other traditional Americans, most Latinos will embrace a societal script centered around strong families and traditional social values. In a debate that goes back to Booker T. Washington and W.E.B. DuBois, many first- and second-generation Latinos are taking Washington's path. They are working hard at the blue-collar level of society so they can send their kids off into a better life.

Contrary to what the progressive elites envision, aligning Latinos with traditional Whites is more doable than uniting millions of Blacks with the same. The real challenge is time. The college professors are already at work with their divide and conquer strategies. Just as Thomas Jefferson and George Washington are perceived to be devils by today's college-educated Blacks, Sam Houston and Davy Crockett will be the next dominoes to fall with college-educated Latinos. If the professors can anger a new influx of younger Latino students over the annexation of Texas *and other acts of white imperialism*, there may be millions of additional Latino converts ready to join the Marxist cause of toppling *the imperialists*. And if the White traditionalists remain stuck on the bumbling path of being pigeonholed into an anti-Latino stance, they will end up playing right into the hands of these professors.

Beyond the Latinos, there is a smaller group of *Brown* Americans who found themselves in the news shortly after Trump was elected in 2016. Studies show Muslims assimilate in America better than they do in Europe.[xlviii] And like Latinos, there is a wide dispersion of culture amongst the 1.8 billion Muslims worldwide.[xlix] Islam, like Christianity during the Dark Ages, is trying to find itself in a world that has changed much since the fall of the Ottoman Empire. Ironically, Islam, Christianity, and Judaism are all bound by the Prophet Abraham and his two sons, Isaac and Ishmael.[l] These three religions originated from the same God. Yet millions of people have been killed in the name of religious purity.

The West hears about the Sunni-Shia split and the millions of deaths that resulted from their infighting. How did the Sunni-Shia split arise? After the Muslim Prophet Muhammad died, there was a dispute over who should be his rightful successor. Some followers felt the line of succession should have been based on blood (Shia), while others felt Muhammad's close confident, Abu Bakr, should have been the rightful successor (Sunni). These groups could not find alignment over this issue, and they have been fighting ever since.[li]

This is a true dilemma with all religions. What Muhammad accomplished in one lifetime was remarkable. Yet, once he perished, the inherent pettiness found in human nature soon reared its ugly head. The problem in the Middle East is not Islam or Christianity or Judaism. These scripts have helped far more people than they've hurt. The real problem lies with the human beings who distort religion to align with their misguided impulses. And it doesn't take long for the fighting to begin once the divine founder exits a worldly existence.

Like Christianity and Judaism, Islam carries with it hope and ambiguity. Muhammad came from a merchant-class family, so it is possible Western-style capitalism and Islam are compatible.[lii] But many hurdles still remain between the two cultures. Islam allows private property ownership but has not fully reconciled the concept of charging interest (*riba*).[liii] It is difficult to embrace a twenty-first-century market economy when one must overcome the religious barrier of meeting a banker wearing a *niqab*.

Most troubling of all perhaps, the Qur'an has clearly defined rules about Islam coexisting with Christians and Jews. There is little gray area with Qur'anic scripture that instructs outsiders to either convert to Islam or pay a tax.[liv]

Islam, like Christianity during its dark spell, may require decades of self-introspection before it fully reconciles itself to the new realities of modernity. True, there are many great Muslims contributing to the success of the US today. In addition, there is little downside in allowing more Westernized Muslims to immigrate to America. But in this time of regional and religious uncertainty, why would the progressive elites be so anxious to import millions of uneducated refugees from war-torn countries like Syria?

Whereas Muslim women in the Middle East are forced to cover their faces, teenage girls in the West find little dilemma in posting nude selfies on Instagram. How do two such radically different cultures come together without first expecting conflict and chaos? Shouldn't we get our own affairs in order as a country before we invite a guest who is battling its own set of problems?

Why not let Western Europe be the Islamic mass-migration experiment of the twenty-first century? It probably won't take m u c h longer for the historians to decide whether German Chancellor Angela Merkel was an enlightened saint or a twenty-first-century do-gooder fool.

When the standardized test scores for K-12 education come out, there is always one demographic that seems to stand out.

What do Southeast and Pacific Rim Asians bring to the United States? Low child out-of-wedlock rates, a strong work ethic, and a predisposition to do well in school. One would think these qualities would align with the Republican Party, but we know this is not the case today. The college professors are very good at reminding Asian Americans about xenophobic Whites and World War II internment camps.

There are, however, fault lines beginning to emerge between the Democrats and Asian Americans. The Democrat Socialists are nervous about the propensity of this demographic to earn big salaries. And the diversity police are uncomfortable with the disproportionate amount of classroom seats Asian students fill at many of our prestigious universities. How long can the social engineers continue to discriminate against Asian Americans in college admissions? How long can colleges like Harvard use "personality tests" to select its students?

The college admissions departments need to stop playing politically correct games. If one ethnic group occupies 75 percent of the student body at Harvard, God bless them! It would mean other US students should study harder. Americans should be united by one set of rules and the pursuit of excellence. Instead, the elites have pitted us all against each other. The United States is exceptional because it is the one country that has shown it can unite millions of human beings by ideas that transcend ethnic origin. Before the era of White guilt and progressive *empathy*, immigrants didn't come to the US for freebies. People like my parents came to the US because it was the one place they could pursue their full, God-given potential. Why are we allowing the social engineers and race baiters to divide us by identity politics and double standards?

There are approximately 7.5 million citizens in Hong Kong who understand their days as a democracy are numbered. It may only be a matter of time before China wraps its dictatorial tentacles around this highly innovative group of human beings.

The Wall Street Journal wrote that the United States should consider opening its doors to Hong Kong visa holders.[lv] According to WSJ sources, *67% of Hong Kong residents speak average, good, or very good English, and one in five adults planned to launch a business within the next three years.*[lvi] Why wouldn't Americans want to offer this type of guest permanent refuge in the greatest civilization in human history?

Our Hong Kong mass-migration plan is bold and destroys the progressive notion that traditional Americans are xenophobic. America will always be able to find a place for talented human beings who speak English. In addition, immigrants who live next door to tyrants and cartels are not easily fooled into believing the falsehood that humanity is on the cusp of embracing widespread harmony. Moreover, human beings who witness tyranny in their own backyards are less likely to be duped into picking central planners over freedom fighters. If our country finds an opportunity to gain thousands of highly educated, hardworking, and entrepreneurial people who speak English, we should open our doors and say, "Welcome!"

Do the modern Greeks hide the Parthenon because their ancient rulers practiced pederasty? Do today's Italians talk about razing the Colosseum because slaves were fed to the lions? No society can guarantee perfection or happiness to all. If traditional Americans can find a way to *divorce* their toxic partners, like-minded Blacks, Browns, and Whites can begin the first steps toward having a unified country. And should the United States rid itself of the intellectual fascism and political correctness that festers in every corner of society, our country could find itself in the incredible position of attracting *millions* of talented and hardworking Latinos and Asians who are being chased away by bullies.

The United States could be on the brink of widespread civil unrest. In a revolutionary environment, Asians and Latinos could find themselves in the unbelievable position of deciding the final outcome in the United States of America. This type of prediction isn't based on conjecture; it's based on math. If a traditional mass movement loses 30 percent of Whites and 95 percent of Blacks, there is only one demographic left to decide which direction the marriage will take.

If we simplify our conversation to being on one of two teams—Team Red or Team Blue—it is hopefully becoming clear what the differences are between *each team*. In the context of a mass-movement strategy, traditional Americans need to create a different discussion than the narrative of racism and xenophobia. Expanding on the Hong Kong emigration plan would represent a good first step. In fact, this type of discussion should become an immediate priority.

Here at home, we need to begin a new conversation with common-sense Latinos, Muslims, Asians, and also, the seven million American Jews.[lvii] Each one of these groups is amazingly voting against the Republicans at a near 2-1 margin. How long can this type of spread continue before the clock runs out on the original defenders of liberty and limited government?

There is another group voting Democrat at a 2-1 clip: our kids and grandkids.[lviii] Millions of younger Whites believe open borders and universal outcomes are possible in the natural human order. To many millennial Whites, the word "socialism" brings with it a warm, fuzzy image of Uncle Bernie. Conversely, the word "capitalism" conjures up darkness and images of Dick Cheney. Quite frankly, I don't know if today's millennials, in a majority capacity, have the fortitude to dig themselves out of a hole that began in the 1960s and proliferated after the radicals monopolized academia, Hollywood, and government. On a per capita basis, studies can't show what many parents know in their gut: their kids were often raised in soft and confused environments with very little to believe in beyond saving the planet from capitalism and fighting against social injustice.

Today, there are millions of younger Whites destined for low-paying jobs, living at home with their parents, or living on the streets. I can't remember a time when there were so many twenty-something-year-old Whites holding cardboard signs at street intersections. Look at the rates of working-age Whites who have given up finding a job or the number of Whites who are on permanent disability in their twenties and thirties. Look at the suicide rates of these young Americans. And look at how many of them will die using hardcore drugs.

Younger Whites don't know if they are socialist or capitalist, innocent or guilty, or even male or female. A majority of Generations Y and Z will not understand what it means to live life for a cause greater than trying to fight the confliction that comes with being *privileged*. This sociological reality brings us to a potential gut-wrenching decision. To rescue our kids from their handlers, we may first have to let them move out of the house without any contact or support from us. We may have to step back and allow them to move in with the wrong people before they figure out who truly has their best interests in mind. Millions of younger Whites may have to discover the true meaning of life by living in the same neighborhoods as Colin Kaepernick, Michael Moore, and Alexandria Ocasio-Cortez.

The American dream doesn't have to be limited to student debt loans, privilege, and guilt. Just as we initiated a real conversation with Blacks and Browns, now is the time to begin a discussion of hope and redemption, with ourselves, our kids, and our grandkids.

Chapter 6: Divided and Conquered White

Those who see their lives as spoiled and wasted crave equality and fraternity more than they do freedom. If they clamor for freedom, it is but freedom to establish equality and uniformity.

—Eric Hoffer

Where do we start with "White" America? Let us begin by putting ourselves in the mind of a progressive *intellectual.* Envision a global community without borders, guns, or inequality. How would we begin the process of constructing such a utopia? We would first seek to disregard every American tradition and begin from scratch. The United States and its *White* traditions represent the biggest impediment in finding global harmony and universal outcomes. Who has the most guns? The United States. Who has the most hegemony over the global community? The United States. Who perpetuates the greatest levels of inequality and social injustice? You guessed it: White people living in the US.

How would a modern-day Saul Alinsky sow doubt and confusion onto the dominant White culture? He would begin by indoctrinating their young and shaming the old into submission. How would a leftist agitator break up traditional families? By marginalizing mothers and fathers and eliminating the lexicon of gender pronouns like Sir, Mrs., mom, dad, boy, and girl. How would a George Soros globalist destroy traditional White influence? By dividing the American citizenry into myriad factions and flooding the country with newcomers who aren't emotionally vested to the original founding principles of the US Constitution.

White Americans across every spectrum of society have been divided and nearly conquered into a perpetual state of disrepair and division. Today, we are fighting against each other across nearly every demographic:

- Male versus female.
- Blue-collar versus white-collar.
- Young versus old.
- Rural versus urban.

Of all the battles going on within the various subgroups, we know the *real* enemy in the progressive plot is the toxic White male. In today's intellectual climate, it is difficult to believe a White male has a right to complain about anything:

- He has gained immense power and privilege by pillaging the resources of other cultures.
- His skin color is the same as every former president but one.
- He is the chairman on nearly every corporate board.

The sons and grandsons from the heroes of yesteryear face a new enemy who is far more lethal than an Adolf Hitler or Joseph Stalin. Instead of dying an immediate death from a bullet, the White male is at risk of dying a slow death from a disease that begins and ends with mere words. In today's hostile environment, he essentially has three choices:

- He can apologize for his previous privilege.
- He can become a Democrat.
- Or he can switch genders.

The social engineers are hard at work trying to teach school-aged boys how to become less aggressive and more tolerant. The broader goal is to shame the White male identity into not judging other cultures that are deemed to be disadvantaged. Making judgments about other cultures, of course, perpetuates racism, xenophobia, and global conflict.

The new rite of rigorous passage into manhood for twenty-first-century males isn't about transforming primitive impulse into a conscious state of courage, self-reliance, and love of country. Today's rite of passage is about learning how to discard the *nationalist, racist, and privileged* behaviors of the past. The role models for younger males are no longer policemen, firefighters, and Navy SEALs. These masculine heroes of the past are simply too toxic to be considered positive role models today.

My construction career began with men who defeated global tyrants and ended with adult boys who never learned that showing up on time, doing what you say you're going to do, and doing things you *don't want to do*, transform primitive male minds into reliable husbands, strong fathers, and the future guardians of liberty. White males from previous eras built an exceptional civilization with a can-do spirit that arose from unprecedented levels of freedom and the individual toughness that came from taming a vast frontier. Even the most ardent feminists would have trouble denying the White males from yesteryear were the primary architects and builders of the freedoms we enjoy today. These men designed a blueprint to bring upon the greatest degree of science, medicine, architecture, and engineering the world had ever known. Yet today, they can do nothing right. Thousands of former heroes are now looked down upon as disgraced "racists, misogynists, and colonialists."

I suspect many younger women are also witnessing the tragic fall of the confident White male. Trying to find a stable, mature, and masculine life partner is not an easy task in an environment where boys seem to remain boys well into adulthood. The experts say thirty is the new twenty. But I would suggest that both females and males in their twenties begin the marital lockdown process sooner rather than later. Whether it is the immature male who sends *dick pics* before the first date, or the insecure female with *daddy-daughter* issues, the talent pool of stable White men and women in the United States is shrinking fast.

Today is an exciting, yet stressful, time to be a woman in a global reality where brains and people skills matter more than physical strength. While there will still be male holdouts from a bygone era, there are tremendous opportunities for Western women that did not exist only two decades ago. But there is also great risk and unnecessary turbulence being fostered in a progressive environment that seeks to repair thousands of years of gender interaction in one quick and easy stroke. Opening the doors to sexual equality between men and women, for instance, has changed the way young women think of themselves. In today's hypersexualized world, girls, even at an elementary school level, measure their identities against those famous females who are clever and beautiful enough to sexualize God-given talents into multimillion-dollar business models.

Before recent times, young women selected future mates based on the parameters set by the one male who loved them free from sexual intent: their dad. Today, however, many White adolescent women lack a strong, loving, and masculine paternal figure. As with most Black families, there is a good possibility the White father isn't up to the task of providing guidance, unconditional love, or even availability to his daughter(s). In this regard, the family structures of Blacks and Whites are converging in a new pop-culture climate that glorifies songs like WAP to every eleven-year-old girl in America.[1] Can any of us contemplate being a teenage girl in this progressive era of fatherless homes and rampant sexual objectification of young women?

With the new norms in place, it will be a rough ride for those twenty-first-century females who don't possess the inner fortitude to keep up with the Kardashians. Instead of building a model of femininity from the inside looking out, the intellectuals and their cohorts in pop-culture are reconstructing a new female identity shaped by rappers and radical college professors. Today, there are four-year college majors that can articulate—in extraneous detail—the origination of male dominance, how such dominance has led to unnecessary wars and inequality, and what must be done to rescue humanity from this evil. Women are being taught at the universities to defeat men, and to even hate them, in the monumental Marxist struggle to find economic equality in the workplace.

I am not suggesting women have found societal equilibrium with men. Today's women from *every ethnic origin* have the obvious right to continue fighting for greater rights. But the gender puzzle is more complicated than taking the earnings of every male and female, dividing by two, and then pitting today's future mothers and fathers against each other until the numbers align. The final result for many educated young women is the perception that true happiness can only be found

---

[1] Cardi B, Featuring Megan Thee Stallon, "WAP" acronym for "Wet-Ass Pussy," Atlantic Records, August 2020, digital download, #1 Billboard Hot

when the glass ceiling is broken; as if spending an entire life climbing the corporate ladder has become more important than man, woman, and child being vested in a lifelong compact.

Rather than debating how today's men and women can find greater happiness and balance at home and at work, the intellectuals and their minions are diminishing the most important partnership in human history. White males are essentially being asked to hate who they are, and Western women are being reduced to *bitches*, *hoes*, and Marxist trailblazers. Both are in desperate need of a mass movement that has the revolutionary power to unwind decades of guilt and indoctrination.

Beyond gender, there is also a profound disconnect occurring between rural and urban Whites and blue- and white-collar Whites. As a former construction worker, I often left a jobsite and walked directly into a classroom environment. It was always fascinating going from a 40' ladder in thirty-five mph wind gusts to the theoretical setting of a progressive class. It was at those moments, however, that I could best see the contempt and arrogance that some college-educated Americans have for those blue-collar Whites who vote for Republicans.

Disturbingly, Whites without college are far more likely to be unmarried than those who attended college.[lix] Neighborhoods that once housed future generals, CEOs, and presidents are under siege from opiates, depression, and suicide. Older blue-collar males are under attack for being toxic, unenlightened, and privileged, and their sons are stressed out trying to figure out why life seems to have so little meaning. Contrary to what the academics believe, working-class Whites aren't voting Republican out of ignorance, hate, or globalization. Working-class and rural Whites are desperate because they have lost their cultural standing in society. Before the crusade against traditional males, blue-collar men found pride in teaching younger males how to use tools and wit to accomplish difficult tasks. Until recently, there was equal standing in going to college, learning a skilled trade, or serving in the military. In centuries past, a white-collar engineer respected the blue-collar laborer even though both came from two completely different educational backgrounds. Importantly, both may have served in the military together.

Now, however, the distance and divide between blue- and white-collar Whites has little point of connection. Blue-collar parents are often looked down upon for being *deplorable* and *uneducated* not only by the leftist elites, but by their *enlightened and college-educated* children.[ix] White-collar and urban Whites with college degrees are likely to view blue-collar and rural Whites as angry, sexist, and racist human beings who are stupid enough to vote for Republicans. Here's how a typical professor would intellectualize why blue-collar and rural Whites tend to vote for Republican candidates:

Professor #1 to students:

Twenty-first-century globalization and urbanization have adversely impacted rural and working-class White America. Technological advances and corporate offshoring have reduced the economic standing of lower-income Whites in a disproportionate manner. Working-class White people are losing out in a global economy, and there are political actors who have been successful in projecting such economic and demographic anxieties onto newly arrived immigrants.

Professor #2 to students:

The capitalists have cleverly created a political compact with economically challenged White people at the expense of African

Americans. By demonizing people of color, they have created a cultural reality where fear and a perception of White privilege have united the White peasant with the White master. In this set of circumstances, lower income Whites are voting against their own economic self-interest.

Coming from a real blue-collar environment, I could easily understand how the professors were using academic nonsense to typecast blue-collar Republicans as racist, stupid, and xenophobic. To many of my classmates, however, the above logic made perfect sense. Unlike most blue-collar Whites, younger, upper class Whites live a comfortable life in a globally connected world. Their helicopter parents made a good living, and today, the adult children are accustomed to nicer restaurants and traveling abroad. If this demographic of younger Whites somehow escaped the liberal guilt trip while in college, their parents probably had the right connections to ensure a good career path to cities like San Francisco, Boston, or New York. While in these "cool" cities, younger Whites with college degrees will see the best aspects of cultural diversity because everyone else around them is also smart and motivated. In cities like Austin and Seattle, the career paths of younger, urban Whites are in near-perfect alignment with the progressive message of embracing diversity and voting for Democrats.

This subculture of affluent, younger Whites often grew up in environments where individual identities were forged from carefully scripted parental plans that managed personal risk in fine detail. Big companies will do everything possible to recruit the brains of college-educated Whites through the proliferation of workplace fitness centers, impressive lunch menus, and bring-your-parents-to-work holidays. Corporate America wants the intellect and pedigree of the best Generations Y and Z have to offer, and they have found ways to merge personal insecurities into *socially responsible* work environments.

It is true these younger Americans are fueling a technological revolution that is no less profound than what other Americans achieved in the past. But unlike previous generations, this group remains well insulated from the worst aspects human nature has to offer. Younger, professional, urban Whites generally aren't exposed to the possibility of having a gun pointed to their face unless they make a wrong turn on their way home from a downtown Weezer concert. These educated and idealistic Whites have bought into the globalist platform that borders don't matter, and that all cultures are created equal.

Traditional White parents and grandparents are struggling to understand how a Bernie Sanders could have had so much appeal with their college-educated kids and grandkids. While older Whites can blame Sanders and his Marxist rhetoric, *we* should begin by pointing the finger at ourselves. We put our jobs and making money ahead of family time. We allowed the national debt to increase to unsustainable levels. We allowed the 1960s radicals easy access to our public schools, universities, and even our living rooms. We sat back and watched the cost of a degree triple, and we never questioned why the politicians ever got into the business of college loans in the first place.

Older, traditional Whites also share culpability in allowing the 2009-10 housing bubble to occur. As fiscal conservatives, we quietly allowed the baby-boomer presidents to expand the federal government into the home mortgage business. When the government began competing against financial institutions for business, private banks found themselves pitted against easy loans and zero-down payments. But we played along with the pie-in-the-sky rhetoric anyway, believing Presidents Bill Clinton and George W. Bush when they said the federal government could build an "ownership" society.[lxi]

What was the result of the government distorting the residential real estate market? A housing bubble that wiped away billions of dollars in personal net worth. Throw in the aftermaths of 9/11, the Great Recession, weak public schools, social media, and biased universities, and we can begin to understand why millennials are being drawn to a "Democrat Socialist" message that promises to project every defect from the past onto millionaires and billionaires.

Today, millennial, college-educated Whites are moving into higher positions on Wall Street and in Washington, D.C. They are seeking to fill the void, and perhaps lessen the guilt, that comes with being "privileged." As young adults, millennials in positions of power want to change the world in the image painted by their academic and pop culture role models. These conflicted Americans want to displace the guilt and apathy of being born White into a global cause that seeks harmony with other cultures and the planet.

I am respectfully asking White Generations Y and Z to truly contemplate both sides of the human nature question. Are my writings blinded by age, bias, and privilege, or am I forecasting the perfect storm for America and Western civilization? What will happen to your future if life is based on hard power, domination, and regeneration? How will your quality of life be impacted when older, traditional Americans die off and potential bad actors seek to fill the heavy hand of the twentieth-century cowboy? What will be your future fate if non-Whites eventually align together against the *privilege* that has been typecast onto all White people?

Thousands of White baby boomers retire in the US every day, and the federal debt is rapidly approaching thirty trillion dollars.[lxii] Who's going to be stuck with the final tab if the propaganda value of "White privilege" boomerangs back into the universally held belief that *privileged* Whites should pay back their own bill? The older Whites won't be paying off the debt they made. Many of them will be dead before any difficult austerity measures have to be taken. The Blacks aren't going to pay the debt either because they don't have the money. And what about Browns—are millions of Latino and Asian Americans going to pony-up trillions of dollars in debt that was authored primarily by Whites?

History is littered with doom-and-gloom prophets who proved to be very wrong in their dystopian assumptions about the youth of their era. Today, however, our country is in a philosophical no man's land between Karl Marx and Thomas Jefferson, and it won't matter who wins the presidency in 2020—the turbulence, dysfunction, and national debt will continue to escalate in the United States.

When will *educated* Whites begin to realize they were *played* by many of their college professors? Why does it seem like Donald Trump is the last remaining White person willing to speak up against the intolerant fascists? I acknowledge the personal risks that come with talking this way. Communicating beyond the constraints of political correctness is a good way to be permanently labeled a Ku Klux Klan sympathizer or a Neo-Nazi convert. But it is time to set aside the guilt by association. Whites are on the verge of being divided and conquered into a state of irrelevance.

I am suggesting *we* need to experience our own "woke" moment as the heirs to the greatest social compact ever made in human history. Our ancestors built something great, and we are allowing a tremendous civilization to rapidly decline with silence, guilt, and indifference.

How many thriving Black democracies exist in the world? How important were the Whites in assisting Pacific-Rim countries sprout their democratic roots? Not every culture has what it takes to defend liberty from tyranny. Before the era of cancel culture and privilege, Whites took pride in their democratic heritage. If Whites can't muster the confidence to begin having real discussions soon, they could lose everything.

And when they fall, their democratic friends and allies will be in great jeopardy.

I want to return to our previous conversation about men and women. Earlier in this book, I painted a picture of my father as the perfect immigrant. Unfortunately, my dad didn't always come home at dinnertime. It wasn't until later that I realized he sometimes missed dinner because he was out with a girlfriend. My mother was the true rock of the family, but like many women, she received too little credit. How does this happen, one may ask—how is it someone like my mother was relegated to second-tier status even though she was the backbone of the family?

If today's Whites don't seek real solutions to these types of difficult questions, there will be no sustainable mass movement occurring in the United States. Using my mother's example, White women will gravitate to the Marxists because having an "empathetic" plan is a better alternative than being clueless. Just as White Generations Y and Z will pick Black Lives Matter over their parents if the latter can't escape the guilt by association that comes with being *privileged.*

How can Whites find unity without joining right-wing hate groups? How do today's millennials go about finding hope and happiness in a world that seems to have so little meaning? How do blue- and white-collar Whites come to recognize they are both *equal* contributors to the future success of America? And how do male and female Whites get past the Marxist nonsense that the ideal life can only be measured by fighting income inequality in the workplace?

By waking up before it is too late.

It's time for Whites to rediscover themselves before they lose their great country. I don't see the dynamic of "White guilt" or "White privilege" changing without a completely different discussion on race. Whites can find their confidence again without being ignorant fools, but they need to understand they are at a defining moment in history. If they continue to run away from who they are in such a reckless and guilty fashion, hostile actors will eventually seek to fill the void that comes from being a weak and divided people. If we continue to allow our kids and grandkids to be so easily poisoned into hating who they are, who will lead the fight of being the most reliable defenders of freedom and democracy? American Blacks? American Browns?

Maybe in the future, but not today.

If Whites can't find the confidence to begin real conversations beyond the circular and nonsensical path that follows words like *racism, sexism, diversity, multiculturalism, and privilege,* they will eventually be conquered into submission. Conversely, if Whites can find a way to harmonize their past and present into a future path of self-confidence and optimism, more Blacks and Browns will pick the freedom path of George Washington over the utopian path of Bernie Sanders.

We have learned from the Tea Party that traditional Whites can't fight back against the fascists by being afraid. It's time to change tactics. Let's stop with the incessant need to apologize for being *privileged and racist.* Enough of the sensitivity and diversity workshops! Let's open up a real dialogue that discusses the ramifications of either uniting as Americans *by character and culture* or breaking up the country by geography.

Should different conversations begin occurring in America, older Whites may risk their finances, and even their lives, if younger Whites, Browns, and Blacks find the conviction to speak out against relativism disguised as empathy, ignorance packaged as enlightenment, and fascism promoted as virtue. But if younger Whites stay guilt ridden, Blacks continue to knock down monuments, and Browns move closer to the progressive and Marxist Whites, older traditional Whites will simply fade away knowing the time of the optimistic American cowboy has passed.

We are getting closer to discussing mass-movement tactics and revolutionary theory. But we have one last fault line to visit. In 2015, there was a major battle decided without any formal debate.[lxiii] Psychology tells us sexuality and gender are complex processes that play out in the minds of every human infant. Today, children in the West are being besieged with a cultural narrative that glorifies sexual and gender exploration at nearly every turn. Elementary-aged students are being taught that gender is a fluid choice, and anyone who disagrees is *homophobic.*

As the kids grow older, the new gender narrative of the twenty-first century will likely expand. *Are girls really girls and boys really boys, or have we all been playing in a rigged game where the human beings with penises created a set of patriarchal rules intended to dominate the human beings with vaginas?* This type of intellectual lunacy is already playing out at many of our universities. If one believes men and women are inherently different and children benefit from such biological and cultural differences, where does the traditionalist go in today's world of gender-neutral pronouns?

Republicans were nowhere to be found when this battle was being waged. In another brilliant overnight reversal, unbridled sexual exploration has become the new norm, and those who question the new rules have become the patient with a diagnosable disorder. While many Americans have concluded the battle with gender and sexuality is over, the opposite may just be true. The case on gender and sexuality needs to be reopened before the divorce proceeding begins.

Chapter 7: The New Gender Galaxy

Either you are homophobic, or you are a human—you cannot be both.

—*Abhijit Naskar*

Anthropology tells us men were hunters and women were gatherers for thousands of years. Males were physically stronger in a world that favored muscle over brains. Men fought in wars, so boys were trained to be warriors and hunters. Human infants required nurturing to offset the incredible burden that comes with a rational mind in an unexplainable world. The most logical choice for this important role was the biological mother who was one with the child for nine months. The best choice to be the physical protector of the child was a strong male with DNA connection to the child. A social compact was thus made: females provided emotional security to their children and males provided physical security.

Today, the leftist radicals are in a race against time to overcome White-male dominance at every level of society. Academics have reached the conclusion that gender is merely a state of consciousness manipulated by patriarchal traditions. The LGBTQ community has convinced millions of us to believe traditional marriage and gender patterns are outdated and discriminatory. And the millennials are all-in with this new societal arrangement. Nowadays, if a twenty-two-year-old guy doesn't have what it takes to have sex with a girl, he can simply jump into bed with his bigender roommate.

There are dozens of gender and sexual orientation possibilities up for consideration today; how does the traditionalist make sense out of the fact another gender galaxy was recently discovered? Let's take a look at some of the new human identities that make up our twenty-first-century gender reality:

- Agender: A person with little or no connection to a specific gender.
- Androgynous: A gender expression with both elements of masculinity and femininity.
- Bigender: A person who fluctuates between both female and male identities.
- Bisexual: A person who is physically, emotionally, and/or sexually attracted to both men and women.
- Crossdresser: A person who dresses and behaves in a way characteristic of the opposite sex.
- Gender Fluid: A person whose daily feelings fluctuate between a man and a woman.
- Gender Variant: A person who does not conform to the gender-based expectations of society.
- Intersex: A term for people born with a combination of female and male physical traits.
- Metrosexual: A term for a man with a strong aesthetic sense beyond the cultural norms.
- Pansexual: A person who experiences sexual, romantic, and/or physical attraction to all gender identities.
- Skoliosexual: A person who is primarily attracted sexually, romantically, and/or emotionally to

some genderqueer, transgender, and/or non-binary people.

• Transgender: A person whose gender identity and/or gender expression differs from what is typically associated with the sex they were assigned at birth.[lxiv]

The new gender definitions are changing in exponential fashion. We now live in a world where it is socially acceptable to believe human beings are biologically predisposed to be male, female, or otherwise. We also live in a culture where previously accepted norms of sexuality and gender are reversing at a rapid pace. An overwhelming majority of Americans have come to accept new gender definitions in ways that would have been unimaginable only twenty years ago.

In writing this book, I had friends and colleagues advise me to leave the issue of gender and sexuality out of the divorce discussion. Here were some typical comments from people whom I respect very much:

• "The real culprit in the debate is Marxism and fascist intellectualism."
• "People may be born gay. I'd rather have two loving gay parents than two crackhead heterosexual parents."
• "By targeting the issue of gender and sexual orientation, you're going to lose every American under the age of thirty-five."

As I contemplated the United States moving forward as a country, I just couldn't find a way to reconcile the notion that our human existence is based on dozens of gender variations. Nor could I envision a civilization achieving long-term success without being centered around the commonsense notion that a social compact between a mother, father, and child should be the most sacred institution of all.

The gender and sexuality debate of today is a true societal dilemma that goes beyond the US. The Chinese and Russians seem to understand the potential risks associated with moving too fast on longstanding norms that have been a staple of the civilized world for thousands of years.[lxv][lxvi] I'm not sure how long countries like China and Russia will be able to stall the clock on gender expansion, but they are treating the issue with patience and the power of the state. In a better set of circumstances, Americans would also be sitting back and watching how the new sexual norms play out in other Western democracies that pride themselves on "gender tolerance." Like the multiculturalism experiment occurring in Europe, we could have easily stood back and watched how the new gender rules ended up resulting in cities like London and Paris. But it is too late to take such a stance now. Like Europe, Americans are now all-in with the new progressive definitions of gender, sexuality, and marriage.

In a 2015, 5-4 decision, the US Supreme Court ruled in favor of gay marriage.[lxvii] While thousands of gay Americans wept in joy, Chief Justice Roberts wrote in dissent, "The court invalidates the marriage laws of more than half of the states and orders the transformation of a social institution that has formed the basis of human society for millennia, for the Kalahari Bushmen and the Han Chinese, the Carthaginians and the Aztecs...Just who do we think we are?"[lxviii]

So, here we are again, peeling back the sensitive layers of a controversial topic that should have occurred well before the Supreme Court decision came out. This lack of public debate occurs because today's intellectuals will destroy anyone who stands in the way of *liberating* groups that were oppressed by the discriminatory traditions of the past. Taking a step back to analyze the importance of the traditional male and female identity to Western society was never considered, nor was having a rigorous debate about the true origins of sexuality and gender. Is sexuality and gender determined before birth, or are these factors largely determined by environmental circumstances? And why does this matter to society?

If gender and sexual preference are determined before birth, why does *30 percent* of Generation Z in Great Britain today identify as something other than heterosexual?[lxix] Sure, human beings were stuck in the closet before recent times, but the closet was never this big. Something else must be going on beyond genetic variance. Sigmund Freud hypothesized psychosexual development begins in the early stages of childhood. Whether one is reading Freud or speaking to the parent of a *young* toddler, it is mind-numbing observing three-year-old children displaying strong, sexual impulses at such a young age. There must be a complex process on gender and sexuality that takes place in the early stages of human life.

It is also beyond comprehension trying to understand why deviant adults are sexually attracted to young children. Unlike other mammals, human beings have no biological disposition to bear offspring at five years of age. Yet, beyond the realms of our everyday existence lies a world of sexual perversion that is profoundly heartbreaking.

The progressives claim to represent *forward thinking*, but what Miley Cyrus and Cardi B consider to be new and risqué today was tried ten times over two thousand years ago. I admit, the origin of gender and sexuality is complex, but this isn't a situation without historical context. After the Greeks and early Romans fell, every other major civilization tabooed the idea of homosexuality:

- the Hindus
- the Buddhists
- the Jews
- the Christians

- and the Muslims.[lxx]

Why did these cultures place so much emphasis on clarifying two distinct genders?

The *Diagnostic and Statistical Manual of Mental Disorders* spent decades trying to walk the line of whether homosexuality was a disorder or a normal condition that simply required self-acceptance. It seems to make anecdotal sense that some human beings are born with a predisposition to be gay. But it is also a historical fact that gender and sexuality can be influenced by culture. The predominance of homosexuality in ancient Greece and Rome didn't coincide with an escalation in genetic variance; it happened on a widespread basis because the practice was accepted and promoted as a cultural norm.[lxxi] Human infants do not enter the world with a cognitive understanding of their own gender. Is it plausible early childhood dynamics steer infants and toddlers into alignment with their physiological bodies? If this theory is correct, it may explain why people feel like they were "born gay." If gender formation occurs in early childhood, no person is going to remember that exact moment in time when they *became* a *boy, girl, or other.*

The distinction of being "born gay" or "made gay" is really not our issue. Rather, the bold and brazen attempt to move from the single issue of gay marriage in 2015 to a complete redefinition of gender and sexuality five years later is too much, too fast. Why is the West so fixated on prioritizing gender expansion over building a stronger compact between a male, female, and their offspring? Is there a special bond that exists between a father and daughter? Does it make sense that boys benefit from having a strong male role model at home? Do males benefit emotionally by having the unconditional love of their mom? And do girls measure themselves against a strong and feministic role model at home and in life?

I understand the everyday reality that no family is perfect. History is filled with examples of happy, high-achieving people who never met their biological parents. But we're not talking about individual circumstances. We're looking at a myriad of complex sociological arrangements that impact millions of human beings.

Any society that diminishes the institution of marriage between a man and woman does so at its own risk. More profoundly, at what point will the expanding gender list stop?

The LGBTQ community simply overplayed their hand. They got their foot in the door and knocked down the entire house. They have framed the debate on gender as an open-and-shut case, and anyone who disagrees with the new norms is labeled as mean-spirited and homophobic.

Where does the list of genders and sexual preferences go from here? Once it becomes culturally acceptable for the gender-fluid stepfather to go upstairs for a rendezvous with his transgender stepdaughter, what mere mortal will have the power to dig society out of such a hole?

Should five-year-old children be forced to think about dozens of gender choices in kindergarten? The left loves to talk about human rights, but what rights does an elementary-aged child have if they are constantly inundated with an aggressive LGBTQ agenda? Will relaxed standards regarding gender and sexuality diminish the Judeo-Christian covenant between spouses, parents, and children? Will the new norms on sex and gender reduce the incentive for men and women to remain monogamous during child-rearing years?

Unfortunately, these types of debates never occurred either. The present-day phenomenon of the elites being "on the right side of history" has upended any tradition associated with making two genders and traditional marriage the primary staple of Western society. By taking the genie of sexuality and gender out of the bottle with so little debate, five Supreme Court justices have essentially placed the aggressive interests of a small and vocal minority ahead of millions of other citizens. And no one can suggest otherwise without receiving death threats.

Where were the Republicans when the debate on gender and sexuality began? This is the political party that supposedly stands for traditional gender definitions and two-parent families. Instead of fighting back against the radical gays and their friends in Hollywood, the Republicans stood down and allowed longstanding attitudes on gender and sexuality to change without a fight.

Hollywood first opened the curtain with Brokeback Mountain in 2005.[lxxii] The twentieth-century preachers warned breaking traditional taboos associated with sex and gender could open the door to a whole different set of unintended consequences. I'm not trying to advance the idea that sexual purity will ever exist with human beings. Any time someone begins to lecture others on sex and marriage, a hidden skeleton always seems to find its way to the surface. Rather, I am suggesting Americans should have exercised great caution before they were bullied into reversing two thousand years of tradition.

There are simply those conflicts in an advanced society that can't be easily remedied. It is at those moments in a democracy the citizens should be the final arbiter of truth and justice. Complex issues like gender and marriage should have been made by us and not the elites. When society tells its children it is acceptable to become one of a hundred different genders, we are essentially playing Russian roulette with an entire civilization. We are asking immature minds to answer questions the adults haven't figured out yet.

I will never judge a human being for being gay. But just as the *LGBTQ*+ community is asking for *tolerance*, why can't the opinions of other viewpoints be tolerated? How hateful and wrong is it to suggest younger children shouldn't be burdened with complex gender choices so early in life? And why would the most successful democracy in the history of the world change its most important institution without an open and fair trial?

Hopefully, we are beginning to understand the answers to these types of questions. We are living in an era of fascism. The *silent majority* in the United States is too afraid to offend their hostile partner(s) on not only the issue of gender, but every other societal fault line. As Americans, we are reliving the crazed era of McCarthyism all over again. What today's thought police are doing with free speech is not unlike what the Politburo is doing in China. Or what the Ayatollahs are doing in Iran. Or what Putin is doing in Russia. It's time to consider a different strategy than that of the Tea Party. It's time to up the ante and force a real discussion with mass-movement implications.

Chapter 8: The Good, the Bad, and the Ugly

A society that puts equality...ahead of freedom will end up with neither.

—*Milton Friedman*

No mainstream academic or recognized media personality can expose the leftist radicals without secretly pursuing a reputational death wish. The moment any "established expert" tried to write that a male transgender should never be allowed to compete in a female sporting event, an entire career would be destroyed with one stroke of the pen.

I personally witnessed the radicalization process evolve over three decades at the university. We're no longer talking about a handful of 1960s hippies reading Marx and Durkheim in rundown apartment flats in Berkley. We are talking about nearly half of the electorate believing human nature is malleable, communism is a potential virtue, and universal equality should be prioritized over the securement of individual rights.

Today, there are millions of people inside *the system* who have the power to shame and destroy anybody who stands in the way of "progress." In hindsight, the biggest mistake of the traditionalist was allowing the Marxists such easy access into government and academia. The "swamp" has grown beyond control, and even those insiders with common sense are often powerless to take on the leftist dragon who sits beside them.

During the heyday of McCarthyism in the early- to mid-1950s, Republican Senator Joseph McCarthy, and others like him, had the power to destroy reputations and careers. Like all opportunists, McCarthy was able to use soft truths to expand his power to every corner of society. Back then, communist sympathizers, homosexuals, and Blacks were in the crosshairs of men like Joseph McCarthy and J. Edgar Hoover.[lxxiii][lxxiv]

In 1954, however, the dominoes began to fall the wrong way for Senator McCarthy. Joe overplayed his hand, and the public witnessed an *emperor has no clothes* moment in US politics.[lxxv] After an army hearing, McCarthy was exposed as an empty suit who pushed paranoia to consolidate political power. He died three years later at the age of forty-eight from alcoholism and an apparent morphine addiction.[lxxvi] In his last years in the US Senate, colleagues shunned him, and the media ignored him. When he spoke on the Senate floor at the end of his tenure, many of his colleagues would stand up and exit the chamber.[lxxvii] The once-formidable man with near absolute power in Washington D.C. had been exposed as a fraud.

I'm not sure whether there is enough time to experience a McCarthy epiphany again in American politics. McCarthy was essentially a one-man band. Today, there are millions of *social justice* converts with very little to lose in life. They are committed to the cause, and probably won't go away without being forced to leave.

Thomas Jefferson wrote in 1787, "The people cannot be all, and always, well informed. The part which is wrong will be discontented in proportion to the importance of the facts they misconceive; if they remain quiet under such misconceptions it is the lethargy, the forerunner of death to the public liberty…And what country can preserve it's liberties if their rulers are not warned from time to time that their people preserve the spirit of resistance? The tree of liberty must be refreshed..."

According to Jefferson, it shouldn't come as a big surprise the United States is so divided today. If we weren't fighting over social and economic injustice, we'd probably be wasting trillions of dollars trying to find a unicorn. This may simply be who we are as human beings. Powerful civilizations always seem to rise and decline in the natural order of life through decadence, complacency, and ignorance. The question we must ask ourselves today is how long do we want to allow the crazies to have an open and one-sided microphone before we decide to fight back?

America is not destined to follow the same civilizational path of ruin as Rome or Greece. We understand the historical mistakes of the ancients. We have the power of mass communication to discredit the Joseph McCarthys of our era with a simple social media campaign. All we need is to find the right set of mass-movement trigger(s), and we can set into motion an incredible series of history-making events. Just as the progressives are energized with the Black Lives Matter protests today, the traditionalists have the money, power, and guns to create a level of excitement that could make an Occupy Wall Street rally look like child's play.

Aside from a spontaneous set of revolutionary circumstances occurring without warning, I envision five *divorce* scenarios with the possibility of overlap. Although not sexy in nature, there is the chance a new political party and platform could end today's stalemate without the ugliness of a *bad divorce*. As the Democrats and Republicans both wallow in dysfunction, there may be a profound opportunity for the political party that can reinvent itself with a transformative, twenty-first-century platform. Under this type of mass-movement playbook, traditional voters would demand a new political movement that has broader appeal to the entire electorate. The goal with this plan would be to avoid a messy breakup by taking the fuel out of the fire that keeps Marxism alive—class warfare and inequality. In creating a new movement, we would seek to diminish the power of the intellectual and artist classes by making ourselves relevant again in a majority capacity. Further, this approach would formalize our future political intentions in the event the country takes a turn toward a revolutionary path.

This mass-movement strategy would represent a complete overhaul of the GOP with new faces, new ideas, and possibly a new name. If we think about it, the Republican Party has already been taken over by Trump. Why not help Trump expand the coalition even further? And if Trump isn't around, why not regroup and reenergize a new political movement away from the stale faces and policies of the establishment GOP? My emotional attachment to the GOP is simply gone. Republicans have been traveling down a death spiral since Ronald Reagan left office. When a businessman with zero political experience can walk onto the stage from his private jet and defeat the entire Republican establishment, there is a big underlying problem within the overall structure of the organization.

In today's world, what does it even mean to say, "I'm a Republican"? I have no idea what George W. Bush and John Kasich stand for other than being stooges who are easily manipulated by the tactics of Saul Alinsky and Karl Marx. The Republican establishment figureheads stand together with inflexible pride as they get attacked aimlessly by an asymmetrical enemy. They are impotent to fight back because they refuse to set aside the fond memories from a distant past. These men still have not figured out Trump's election victory may have been a rallying cry to blow up the entire Republican establishment.

The second divorce path is where things become more complicated. Let's assume the tension and acrimony continues.

Maybe our problems escalate in ways that can't be anticipated yet. Should the US follow on its current path of dysfunction and debt, reasonable people from both sides will probably say, "Our democracy is broken; we need to try something radically different." Our second scenario is based on the notion of bringing the Republicans and Democrats to the table to discuss how to best separate from each other. This option is based on the idea of holding a constitutional convention to informally outline the ramifications associated with a geographical breakup of the country. Under this strategy, a group of delegates would essentially present a "two America" plan to over three hundred million people, outlining the logistical, military, geographical, monetary, and political ramifications of a geographical split.

The British have shown us complex breakups can be negotiated in the modern world. I don't want to see the United States break into two countries, but what other choice(s) does the traditionalist have if absentee ballots and voting-by-mail schemes create an impenetrable *blue* wall? And what choices will both sides have if today's dysfunction continues to escalate beyond control?

The third and fourth divorce paths are where things get even more dangerous. Without the advantage of hindsight, I imagine two specific scenarios: Trump is in *or* out, but the leftist radicals are still the primary drivers of American culture and politics. These two paths would represent a political environment where the dysfunction in the marriage grows, and neither side is willing to budge. Assuming Trump wins, we would essentially provide a revolutionary road map to a sitting US president. Should Trump lose, we would provide "traditional agitators" a revolutionary manifesto that uses Saul Alinsky-type tactics to instigate and hold the "new and official societal custodians" accountable to their *Democrat Socialist* playbook.

The fifth divorce scenario could end up being the most plausible of all. When our debt and democratic paralysis reaches a breaking point, no president will have the ability to cut spending and/or raise taxes enough without facing a revolt from the voters. Our final divorce possibility, therefore, assumes millions of Americans may one day demand a "temporary dictator" to radically overhaul what has become a broken democracy. Under this scenario, the *dictator* would have arbitrary power to fix the hot mess that we today call the United States.

Beyond the tensions playing out at home, there is a stealth global contest that will impact billions of people before this century ends. China understands a pure Marxist economy will never generate the wealth and innovation that comes with capitalism. Only those fools in Western academia would believe otherwise. In this era of pseudo intellectualism and fake news, we are too blind to realize China is copying *our* proven playbook—at the very same time *we* are considering their failed Marxist policies from the past century.

China believes a market-based economy in conjunction with an autocratic controlled government will outlast the dysfunctional democracies in the US and Europe. In the end, the winner of today's global debate will use some form of capitalism—that we can be nearly certain of. The real question, however, is one of politics, power, and sovereignty. Will power and sovereignty lie in the hands of individual human beings— the American way? Or will absolute power lie in the hands of a Politburo—the Chinese way?

A revolutionary crisis in the United States would be a dream come true to countries like China. After centuries of being dominated by foreign adversaries, the Chinese people can sense the momentum that comes from rebuilding weakness into strength. Conversely, it can easily be argued the United States is moving in the opposite direction. As a country, we are drowning in division and debt. Worse, our partner is living in an ideological fantasyland that hopes to embrace the very same intellectual nonsense that made China irrelevant in the last century. Compare what Bernie Sanders and AOC are saying in 2020 to what Mao Zedong was saying in 1950—all three of these Marxist misfits could be grouped together as ideological soul mates. I don't think Mao could have imagined in his wildest dreams the United States would one day consider its own *Great Leap Forward* into a world where central planners have more power than the sum of their elected citizenry.

This brings us back to the crux of the divorce. The *dark blue* side of the marriage dreams of a Marxist paradise that has failed in every country it was tried. Their *light blue* cousin is the Democratic Socialist. This latter group envisions a Scandinavian model of peace, tranquility, and high taxes. In fairness to our Nordic friends, these cultures do consistently score high on the UN quality of life indexes. But perhaps it is easier being happy when others are doing the heavy lifting. Why should the Norwegians worry about owning guns with the US military protecting all of Europe? Why would countries like Finland and Norway worry about driving away business innovation with high taxes when they have American companies like Google, Apple, Facebook, and Microsoft parading new products out to market each quarter? And why does a country like Sweden need privatized medicine when pharmaceutical companies like Pfizer, Merck, and Johnson & Johnson are being duly rewarded for their health care innovation by the *US taxpayer*?

Americans have essentially become two very different people, and both sides may be getting closer to a defining revolutionary moment. Democratic socialism can work with small, homogenous populations that value equality over guns and cutthroat competition in the marketplace. But here's the real marital dilemma: The United States can't become a pacifist country while owning the most advanced nuclear weapons in the world. Just as America won't remain an economic powerhouse if its citizens go the European route of prioritizing thirty-five-hour work weeks over leading the world in innovation.

Something must give in what has become a marriage with irreconcilable differences. I respect most Democrats. I can't imagine a purely libertarian or Republican-led world that would allow corporations to be the primary stewards of society. The United States didn't become the most powerful country by only electing laissez-faire Republican presidents. America was built not only by the brilliance of Rockefeller, Carnegie, and Ford, but also on the backs of great men and women who belonged to labor unions. I don't want to break apart from millions of good people who bring so much to the marriage. But just as the Republicans dealt with their Joseph McCarthy cancer in 1954, it may be time for the Democrats to either expose their *devil* or risk being consumed by it.

Do not trust Barack Obama to be the Democrat who unmasks the extremists in his party. This would be akin to trusting the fox to guard the henhouse. Barack Obama is a professional agitator with presidential credentials. I admit, I was surprised to see our ex-president so quiet during Trump's first three years. Obama can be just as loose with the truth as Trump yet come across through the media as introspective, empathetic, and intelligent. Had Trump been a typical GOP president who remained silent, stoic, and guilt ridden—like a Mitt Romney—we would have likely seen much more from our former president on CNN and CNBC.

As we move deeper into a revolutionary environment, expect to see Barack and Michelle Obama make a dramatic return onto the mass-movement stage. Do not expect the Obamas to stop the destruction of monuments, however. Nor will this formidable duo honestly defend previous American presidents who are judged to be *on the wrong side of history*. In Saul Alinsky-fashion, the Obamas will encourage today's protesters to continue their march for *social and economic justice, but* in a *responsible* fashion.

If there is going to be a *marital reconciliation* between Republicans and Democrats, it should never be led by Barack Obama. Instead pay closer attention to the moderate Democrats in Congress, the media, and in the military. These are the Americans who can be more trusted to expose the cancer that resides in the Democrat Party. And these are the voters who may find the courage to switch sides, particularly if we are willing to compromise in how we build our new political coalition.

In the next chapter, we will expand on the "good" divorce option. In creating a new twenty-first-century platform and party, I am asking the traditionalist to think big and long. Don't misconstrue my upcoming ideas as some attempt at backdoor progressivism. The big-picture goal is to initiate a policy debate that is thought-provoking and *revolutionary*.

A new platform and party would essentially seek to:

- Avoid the bad divorce option(s) by building a new ruling coalition of White, Black, and Brown voters.
- Provide Trump the opportunity (should he win in 2020) to rebrand or replace the Republican Party himself.
- Provide a future revolutionary manifesto that would define the "traditionalist" political priorities in the event the "good" divorce shifts to the "bad" divorce.

Our intent moving forward is not about drawing up precise legislation for Congress. Nor do our tactics have to be limited to a Donald Trump or Joe Biden presidency. Whether political players like Trump, Biden, and Obama remain in the game, or are long gone, our next objective is to either find a way to get along or to consider how both sides can break up.

Chapter 9: The Good Divorce

Those who fail to learn from history are condemned to repeat it.

—*Winston Churchill*

The question the traditionalist must consider today is whether a new and bold political party could create a mass-movement environment powerful enough to expose the leftist fanatics in the same way Joseph McCarthy was exposed in the 1950s. Is it possible to construct a *new Republican Party* that can repair our divided country? If so, how would we go about constructing such a new platform and movement?

Last year, I spoke with a retired US senator who was once a Democrat stalwart in the US Congress. Out of respect for him, I will keep his name anonymous. During our conversation, I asked whether the US was facing a geographical split. This ex-Senator suggested "a future crisis, in conjunction with a unifying president" would be the antidote to our current political dysfunction.

After our conversation, I decided to take a closer look at the mindset of a typical twentieth-century Democrat. I also wanted to better understand how the Democrats and Republicans were able to *work together* and get things done without so much hate and acrimony back then. I went back into history from a hundred years ago with the advantage of hindsight. And believe it or not, 2020 is eerily similar to 1920.

Just like then, Americans are o n c e again dealing with a global pandemic, a wealth divide, environmental challenges, racial tensions, and a divided Europe. Our primary challenge today, however, isn't about disease, pollution, race, wealth, or Europe. Our biggest problem is that the Democrats and Republicans are heading on a collision course toward a fast-track divorce.

If we think about our marital situation in greater detail, today's Republicans are not much different than the GOP from 1920. To the dismay of the progressives, the conservative view of human nature has changed very little over the last hundred years and longer. Just like then, most of today's Republicans reject the notion that a handful of elites should have arbitrary power over millions of human beings. Nor do most 2020 conservatives believe human nature is moving closer to equal outcomes and global harmony.

It's really not us who have radically changed the parameters of the marriage; it is our Democrat partner who has veered far beyond the original wedding vows. How many Democrats from 1920 would have allowed millions of refugees to pour across the Southern border with so few questions asked? How many Democrats from a hundred years ago would have accepted an entire reclassification of gender and marriage without a fight? And how many 1920 Democrats would have supported academic safe spaces, participation trophies, and the intellectual premise that all White people are privileged?

While the former Senator wouldn't say so, I believe today's twentieth-century Democrats fear the monster they created in turning a blind eye to the radical college professors. Millennial Democrats have bought into the academic narrative that Western society is rigged, corporations are evil, borders should be opened to millions of refugees, and socialism is a virtue.

Half of the voting public has come to believe the United States, and its traditions, are flawed beyond repair.

I don't know if we can put the *Democrat Socialist* genie back into the bottle without an ugly reboot of society. But we owe it to ourselves, and to our great country, to explore every option before we consider the nuclear option of breaking up the country geographically. The United States is not a third world country with shallow institutions. Is it possible to escape an *ugly divorce* outcome by using hindsight to construct a new political and mass-movement platform that has broader appeal to more Americans? Can we expose the leftist radicals by overhauling our twentieth-century mission statement?

Fortunately, our problems are not just confined to two people stuck in a bad marriage. In a democracy, the goal doesn't have to be about making *everyone* happy. We just need to move the political needle from 50/50 percent to 55/45 percent. In this sense, I am hopeful the lessons from the last century can help us navigate through the problems of today.

At the university, there was one progressive talking point that was often hard to refute:

> Professor:
>
> If there was no progressive movement, there would be no such thing as Social Security. How can any Republican reconcile that Social Security was a bad thing?

When Social Security was enacted in 1935, many twentieth-century Republicans feared the new legislation would bring upon the "death of America." Let's listen to two congressional Republicans from 1935:

"The lash of the dictator will be felt, and
twenty-five million free American citizens will
for the first time submit themselves to a
fingerprint test." —Rep. Daniel Reed, R-
NY[lxxviii]

"...So vast, so powerful as to threaten the
integrity of our institutions and to pull the pillars
of the temple down upon the heads of our
descendants." —Rep. James W. Wadsworth, R-
NY[lxxix]

Unsurprisingly, these conservative congressmen sound a lot
like today's anti-government Republicans. To Reed and
Wadsworth, a huge governmental takeover spelled the death of
democracy and individual liberty. To the progressives,
however, the Social Security Act of 1935 promised a future of
dignity to those who would otherwise grow old without enough
money in the bank.

Eighty years later, who ended up being right? The doom-
and-gloom Republicans or the futuristic Democrats?

They were both right. Yes, *both* sides were right. But they
were also both wrong. Not everyone can save money, and in
1935, the support structure of an extended family was changing
as more rural workers were moving to big cities for factory
jobs. Providing an economic safety net to retired Americans
was an appropriate consideration for an advanced and changing
society. Who today can imagine a world without a retirement
backdrop? Who can honestly argue that early twentieth-century
businesses would have created retirement accounts for their
workers without governmental and union pressure?

Unfortunately for us, the two Republican congressmen
were also correct in their fears that a big government takeover
would lead to further federal encroachment as evidenced by
our trillion-dollar debt obligations today. What good is Social

Security if the federal government goes bankrupt? How many trillions of dollars have been wasted since 1935 as the Democrats (and Republicans) learned they could buy votes by creating more federal programs while borrowing against old ones? The right answer in 1935 was probably the creation of a retirement savings program outside of political control.

We're not looking to begin a discussion about privatizing Social Security now. We saw what happened in 2004 when George W. Bush mixed the word "privatization" with Social Security reform. Our point is that the twentieth-century progressives were probably correct in creating a broader safety net for old age. By staying on the sidelines on the important issue of pension reform, and others like it, the Republicans opened the door to the idea that big government is the answer to every crisis in America.

Our new platform (and party) concept is essentially a first mass-movement step that declares our side will no longer be playing by the previous rules of the establishment Republicans. In addition, the plan is about capitalizing on the present weakness of both parties. Uninformed voters are of the perception Republicans only help rich people. Since most people aren't rich, they identify with the Democrats. Why not create a new movement that aspires to be neutral between employees and employers? Why not discard an outdated brand that is perceived to be elitist?

If one believes today's Republicans and libertarians don't have any room for improvement, let's look at some statistics. In 1965, the CEO/median pay ratio between the boss and his/her workers was about 20:1.[lxxx] Today, that number is closer to 300:1.[lxxxi] In the global economy, fewer than one hundred people have more wealth than the bottom three billion.[lxxxii] CEOs seem to have few moral dilemmas in personally making billions of dollars with one hand and paying out twelve dollars per hour with the other hand. Many bosses have little quandary spending a holiday weekend in the

Caribbean while their employees are working a Black Friday away from their families. Established business models that were profitable for decades can become obsolete in months, not years. Yes, the economists can argue innovation increases productivity, and that everything will work out in the end. But the long run is not always nice to a forty-five-year-old worker who spent a lifetime mastering only one or two skill sets.

Today, 60 percent of Americans are on a path to having *zero* savings when they retire.[lxxxiii] If you are rich and think you're safe, you may want to think again. In a democracy, one doesn't want to be on the 40 percent team. The college professors are already training a new band of radicals in how to pursue after-tax money from older Americans with above-average bank accounts.

What is wrong in considering private-sector improvements to 401(k) pension plans? What value is there to a 401(k) if an employee doesn't have the extra funds to build a retirement nest egg? How is it that some profitable companies offer 1:1 matches to their employees, while others who are equally profitable offer nothing?

Why are so many wealthy Americans oblivious to the Marxist alligators lurking just outside their doors? Do the *progressive one-percenters* really think they will find atonement by voting for Democrats? And at what point does one have enough money in life? More importantly, how much wealth does a person need before they begin to see the bigger picture?

I am suggesting we consider getting ahead of today's Marxist-inspired radicals—not only with pension reform but also with wages and health care. If a new political movement can establish a better compact between employees and employers in the workplace, is there a chance we could marginalize today's Marxist academics? More importantly, isn't incentivizing employers to share profits during successful years good public policy?

Our new platform plan isn't about squeezing small-business start-ups with the expectation of profit sharing. Nor should companies be expected to be financially burdened during poor or average years. Our goal, rather, is to think about using different economic and political vehicles that are flexible and more balanced toward finding a greater employee/employer equilibrium.

Let's begin with some low-hanging fruit. Nowadays, someone who makes a million dollars annually by running a small business pays 37 percent in federal income taxes.[lxxxiv] Conversely, someone who makes a million dollars flipping high-end real estate only pays 20 percent in capital gains taxes.[lxxxv] This goes back to Warren Buffet's argument that his secretary pays more in taxes than he does. Why not create an economic platform that says anyone who makes a million dollars must pay the 37 percent tax regardless of how the money was earned? Yes, the establishment Republicans will crow about a previous alternative minimum tax that was wrought with unintended consequences. But how can it be that difficult to implement a uniform level of taxation regardless of how the million dollars was made?

The "death tax" is another issue the Republicans have spun to their political advantage. Most of us don't understand the inheritance tax only applies to an individual with over *11.58 million dollars* in assets.[lxxxvi] Yet, in future election cycles, we can almost predict with certainty the GOP will try to eliminate the *death tax* because the term conjures up images of the federal government trying to confiscate the hundred thousand dollars average-Joe planned on leaving to his kids when he passes away. Instead of playing games with the public, give the very wealthy two choices upon death: Either pay taxes on any wealth accumulated beyond a certain threshold or give the money to a charity of their choice. Why would any society want to see a billionaire's kids inherit five billion dollars? And what billionaire would be stupid enough to hand their hard-earned money over to the federal government in lieu of a private charity?

In what could best be described as an Andrew Carnegie approach to advancing society, the choice of giving billions of dollars to a charity versus giving the money to the government would incentivize the wealthiest citizens to put their talents to work for all of society. Even liberal billionaires are smart enough to understand giving money to the government is like throwing wealth into a black hole. And policies such as eliminating tax loopholes and forcing billionaires to give back to society are political winners with most voters.

Now, let's move the needle a little further. Should company owners be required to post their CEO/median employee pay ratio? This type of legislation is already in place for some public companies,[lxxxvii] but the guidelines are easy to manipulate due to the myriad of loopholes that can be used to disguise CEO compensation. In addition, today's laws don't require privately held companies to display this data. Why not support a political platform that requires *all* businesses to show such information? This mechanism would allow employees the right to go online to compare their boss's pay ratio to other owners in the same field.

Again, hear me out. When my business began to gain traction, I had a great team of people who believed in me. As the company grew, I always promised *the team* we would find the "Promised Land" of making big money and being the best at what we did. After years of growing pains, that big day finally arrived. At the time, my company had thirty employees, a million dollars in leftover profits, and no debt. What was the *right* thing to do with the money? Sure, I was the founder and sole individual responsible for litigation, problems, and payrolls, but what about the team? Without them, the million dollars wouldn't be sitting in the bank.

I ended up keeping half and giving the other half away as year-end bonuses. This may not sound like the stuff of Robin

Hood, but keep in mind I assumed ownership of a company with three-hundred thousand dollars of debt. For years, our competitors predicted employees would become bitter once the bonuses came to an end. But the doomsayers were wrong. Even in the down years of 2009-10, our entire company took pay cuts with no bonuses. There were few defections or morale problems during the Great Recession, and over time, our company attracted the best talent in the industry. We became a juggernaut in our respective field, and that first million-dollar profit-sharing program multiplied exponentially.

By the end of my career, the CPA was returning millions of dollars back to a great team of people nearly every year. And our business wasn't some kind of Fortune 500 company. Yet, each successful year, we had to warn the local banks to carry millions of dollars in cash on hand for the second Friday of each December.

I'm not looking for a pat on the back here. As a leader who built a committed team, I simply couldn't rationalize the idea of keeping all the profits for myself. And in taking this approach, other ripples began to occur throughout an entire industry. Before our company began the trend of large, year-end bonuses, the industry norm around Christmas was to hand out Wal-Mart gift certificates. Once word got out about the bonuses, however, the Wal-Mart debit cards took a backseat to nice end-of-year profit-sharing checks at many of my competitors. No, my gratuitousness wasn't always appreciated by other company owners. But as I reflect in time, sharing big profit years in such an unusual fashion was the most rewarding business decision I ever made, bar none.

There should be more to being a CEO than simply keeping shareholders happy. Barack Obama already started things when he told business owners, "You didn't build that..."[lxxxviii] The libertarian CEO who hates intrusion in the marketplace is likely to be the same person whose Yale-educated children revere Bernie Sanders. If the traditionalist doesn't figure out a way to make pay, health care expenses, and pensions more equitable, the next wave of lefties will have no problem piercing IRAs, bank accounts, and safe-deposit boxes. Our twenty-first-century business leaders can be proactive, or they can face the ugly alternative at their own peril.

I often think about the idea of a new, twenty-first-century labor union model. There should be little debate that unions helped build the middle class of the last century. Unfortunately, many unions have lost their way in today's global economy. As a construction contractor who worked in the unionized factories, I saw the best and worst unions have to offer. While some unions have modernized themselves to be relevant in a fast-moving economy, most remain prehistoric relics stuck in a twentieth-century mindset. To this day, I am shocked many of the steel and auto plants in the Rustbelt States are still in business.

If today's unions are not up to the task of being relevant in a twenty-first-century economy, why not go around them with official public policy? For example, why not mandate by federal law that non-essential workers be paid double time wages on Sundays and holidays at larger companies?

Why not consider legislation that triggers higher employee 401(k) contributions once the boss breaks a 50:1 CEO/median pay threshold? I understand some industries with less-skilled workers and lower wages could skew the median pay formula and vice versa. But can anyone honestly say a company like Amazon shouldn't be forced to contribute a larger 401(k) match when Jeff Bezos pays himself *1.2 million* times the $28,000 median pay of his workforce?[lxxxix]

I have also been thinking about Elizabeth Warren's "wealth tax." Her 2020 campaign plan was to fund Medicare-for-all by levying a tax on accumulated wealth beyond fifty million dollars.[xc] The tax would have to be paid every year—it would not have been a one-time deal.[xci] Warren's proposal would have resulted in an incredible wealth transfer of over 300 billion dollars *every year* forward![xcii]

We'll get back to health care in a moment, but what about the idea of taxing billionaires a *one-time,* after-tax hit that wipes out the student debt bubble? I acknowledge this type of talk sounds like it is coming from a Bernie Sanders campaign rally. But the students didn't create the college debt problem— the adults did. The government should have never involved themselves in student loans in the first place. The result of the politicians moving into the loan business was a big economic bubble and a diluted piece of paper.

With our "billionaire plan," those who honored their student debt loans would be paid retroactively in the same proportion as the students who haven't paid back their loans. In addition, the larger universities would take part in the bailout plan with an endowment tax. The universities went right along with the nonsense that "everybody should go to college." They borrowed heavily to fund expansions, and they devalued the prestige of a college degree by accepting too many unqualified students and professors. Can anyone honestly say a four-year soft degree is worth more than a high school diploma from thirty years ago? How many of today's college graduates are capable of drafting a workplace email that meets only the most basic level of professional scrutiny?

I acknowledge the slippery slope that comes with buying into Elizabeth Warren's billionaire tax logic. Once this door opens, it may never shut. But we may want to consider the future gamble of helping millennials at the expense of billionaires and universities. If society can raise the former out of debt, there is some hope they will eventually find the sense to rejoin their parents and grandparents in the bigger fight of getting the American democracy healthy again.

Now, let's expand our political-platform conversation beyond pensions, wages, and the student debt crisis. Let's begin with the contentious issue of health care.

Health Care

The US spends more in health care than any other country.[xciii] As such, much of the world's innovation in medicine comes from the American free market system. In many respects, the US consumer is subsidizing a disproportionate share of the research and development costs for every other country in the world. With modern technology, humanity may be on the cusp of living to an age that was unthinkable in 1920. However, if the US follows Canada and Europe in nationalizing health care, where will the innovation come from? In this coronavirus era, who can imagine relying solely on governments to find an eventual vaccination? How many medical blockbusters are coming out of the nationally managed health care systems of Canada and Norway?

With a government-run system, money gets lost in the bureaucracy, and there is little incentive to invent billion-dollar medical treatments. With a market system, big corporate profits are made because the individual consumer has no incentive to shop prices. If a typical American has a shoulder injury, he or she doesn't care if the doctor charges five thousand dollars or twenty-five thousand dollars—the patient is primarily interested in timing and convenience. We all know friends who won't visit a doctor unless they are close to death. And we all probably know someone who will go to an emergency room for a pregnancy test.

The final answer in our never-ending health care debate probably lies in a better-defined public/private partnership. Government would have a role in mandating that older and sicker patients don't fall through the cracks of a privately run system. Health care providers could be mandated to be more transparent with their pricing. And both the government and the private sector should incentivize healthy lifestyles, health savings accounts, and price shopping with nonemergency medical situations.

The traditionalist should also avoid buying into the logic that health care should *be equal* in outcome. Even Canada and the United Kingdom have private options, including coming to the US when their government programs are inadequate. Any person who is able-bodied but not seeking work should not have the same level of medical coverage as someone serving in the US military. Forget all the progressive nonsense about equal medical coverage. There should be no societal guilt when a soldier has the Cadillac of medical plans and a prison inmate only has the most basic of health care options.

In addition, the US should prevent other countries from cherry-picking its innovation and charging lower prices to its individual citizens. Why are we paying more for American-made pharmaceuticals than Canadians and Europeans? Should it not be mandated by law that US citizens can't be charged more for *homegrown* prescription drugs than people in other developed nations? Why is the United States allowing so many "socialist" democracies to freeload off the American taxpayer?

Just like 1920, the traditionalist can be proactive on issues like health care, or he/she can let the other side eventually dictate the terms of the debate. If we continue to stall the very complex issue of health care, one thing is nearly certain: the US will end up with a Medicare-for-all solution. And the West could find itself in the unenviable position of relying on China for future health care innovation.

The Environment

In the twentieth century, there were dust bowls exasperated by shortsighted land use policies.[xciv] Today, the primary environmental issue of our era is the threat of climate change. I don't know how much truth there is to climate change being radically impacted by human beings. It's difficult trusting meteorologists who predict weather patterns a week from now, let alone twenty years from now. While in college, I also witnessed how the left senses a tremendous opportunity in linking capitalism to the horrific images of a hotter planet. Future planetary catastrophe and apocalypse induced by greedy millionaires and billionaires solves the spiritual dilemma of a Marxist ideology that lacks a devil, heaven, and hell.

Ignoring the environment because we hate the Marxists and the tree huggers, though, is not the proper way forward. There is visible evidence to support the premise the environment has big problems. Flotillas of plastic and garbage bigger than the state of Texas are floating in the oceans.[xcv] And one doesn't have to be a scientist to understand the carbon buildup associated with several billion additional human beings driving gas-powered vehicles. Why not adopt a new environmental platform that says consumer plastics must be discontinued within the next five years? Why not be the first country to realize a 90 percent alternative automobile market?

Our new platform can be both pro-capitalism and pro-environment. We don't have to play the silly game of picking one at the expense of the other. And we *don't* have to be so easily typecast as the political party of polluters and deniers of science.

Race in America

Today, I can't reference my "Black friends" because this type of "talk" is loaded with racist overtones. This being said, I can't imagine a breakup that leaves behind those Black and biracial Americans who love the United States and simply want to move beyond the politics of skin color.

Contrary to what the media says, *both* Democrats and Republicans want to see Black Americans prosper. The question is how do we get there as a society. Are double standards and trillions of additional dollars in debt the answer in uniting Whites and Blacks? Or are stable families and good schools the best way in offering equal opportunity to all?

The present-day dynamic of *White empathy* combined with *Black wokeness* could be the spark that moves the United States into an *ugly divorce*. I'm under no illusion of what the racial stakes are in this context of time. But I want to clarify again—any future mass movement that prioritizes skin color over individual character will ultimately fail. Should there be a successful realignment in US politics, the "New America" will be Black, Brown, and White.

To those Blacks who are willing to bid goodbye to yesterday, I say, "Come on in, and join the new movement. Be bold, and join traditional Whites in culture, friendship, and matrimony." But to those Blacks, Browns, and Whites who want to remain in the past, fighting the same fights over-and-over again, I offer this future advice—be ready to sleep in the same bed together.

Twenty-First-Century Morality

In this era of secular indifference, should a repurposed United States consider codifying a *twenty-first-century Ten Commandments*? How long can any civilization remain viable when its ten-year-old children have instant access to hard-core pornography on their cell phones?

To this day, no psychologist has discovered a road map for human affairs that is more profound than what the ancients assembled thousands of years ago. Whether one believes in the literal interpretations of the holy books or not, the intellect and foresight of those great minds was incredible. Yet today, we continue to run away from our founding principles to pursue a secularist existence where *equality* is prioritized above every other moral consideration.

Should Karl Marx have more societal standing than Moses, Jesus, Plato, and Locke? Is there any content in the UN Human Rights Manual that has equal footing to the Aristotelian notion that individual balance and virtue are the antidotes to excess and arrogance?

The United States was founded on Judeo-Christian values, the writings of the ancient Greeks, and enlightened European thinkers. If some people are offended by these original covenants, they can easily pick another civilization. As such, a new platform should clarify Judeo-Christian covenants like the Golden Rule and the Ten Commandments are once again welcomed in every public building.

In terms of the gender debate, I acknowledge most of Generations Y and Z have bought into the logic of gender being *fluid*. And I acknowledge the constitutional difficulties associated with reversing the 2015 Supreme Court decision on marriage (Obergefell v. Hodges). But as society blows past the previous two percent benchmark of people being *born* gay, opinions on the origin of gender can hopefully be questioned with science and not just with progressive ideology.[xcvi]

The issue of gender and marriage is simply too important to not be included in a mass-movement platform. Is there anything more vital to the continuation of human society than biologically vested men and women bringing new life into the world as one? And how long do we want to keep giving young children *dozens of gender choices*?

Moving beyond race, gender, and morality, the hope is a bold new manifesto could have the power to break today's red-and-blue stalemate. The goal with this strategy would be to awaken, energize, and unify everyday Americans to fight back against the elites in academia, government, and big business. In essence, we would replace the twentieth-century Republican doctrine with a Trump-like platform that is pro-America, pro-worker, pro-business, and *anti-swamp*. We would radically overhaul education from top to bottom. We would argue why society should be centered around two genders and strong family structures. And most profoundly, we would seek to unify Blacks, Browns, and Whites beyond the divisive allure of identity politics.

I admit this type of thinking may be naïve and overly idealistic. But is there a chance a traditionalist-led mass movement could secure the middle-class center while pinning the far-left radicals into a permanent state of irrelevance? Moreover, could a successful realignment in US politics finally pin the bullseye directly on the source that created our problems in the first place—the intellectuals in academia and their pawns in Washington D.C?

Our goal with the new platform/party concept is not about trying to fool millions of people with a bait-and-switch. It is about rediscovering ourselves to meet great challenges while acknowledging we are inextricably linked to the traditions of the past. Let's step outside our Republican and libertarian playbooks and ask each other some important questions:

- Should a new political platform codify certain elements of Judeo-Christian teachings into official public policy?
- Is today's compact between private workers and multinational corporations too one-sided?
- Should an unexpected health care event have the power to ruin a life savings?
- Is doing nothing about the environment an option in a global reality where plastic bottles and tires are ending up in the stomachs of whales and dolphins?

If the traditionalist stays timid and inflexible, he/she will lose in the same fashion the Republicans did a hundred years ago. But instead of losing out to an FDR, the Republicans could lose to a future anti-American globalist. Why not get ahead of today's dysfunction by thinking big, expanding the tent, and suffocating the true *cancer* in the marriage?

We will know our good divorce plan is taking root should a solid majority of voters move beyond the fault lines that define today's dysfunctional marriage. In addition, we will know our new political movement concept is gaining traction should some of the following conditions begin to occur:

- The GOP, as we know it today, is completely overhauled.
- The leadership of the new "traditionalist" party becomes less White and less male.
- More Blacks begin to publicly denounce progressive politicians and policies.
- The Democratic Party disassociates itself with its cancel-culture extremists.
- More liberal intellectuals and celebrities break ranks in a public fashion.
- Brown Americans move politically closer to traditional Whites.
- More women associate words like "empathy" and "social justice" with ineffective big government and insincere politicians.
- More Americans demand a radical overhaul of K-12 education.
- Public and private universities see a noticeable decline in stature, including bankruptcies, closures, and diminished tenure protection.

What happens if our new political platform/party idea never occurs? What are our options if today's tensions escalate? We will know our marriage is taking a turn for the worse should some of these circumstances play out:

- A Trump loss or win in 2020 elevates the divorce fault lines.
- Traditional red states turn blue, creating a potential permanent imbalance of national political power.
- Individual states blatantly disregard the federal government and the US Constitution.
- An unexpected crisis results in widespread civil unrest.
- A federal debt crisis occurs with real-life consequences.
- A persistent escalation of racial protests and violence takes root in more American cities.
- States, counties, and cities attempt to unilaterally secede from the US.
- Browns move politically and culturally closer to Blacks and Marxist Whites.
- The US military breaks its code of silence on politics.

If America takes a turn for the bad, what is our Plan B? Most of us are not looking to see the US split geographically, but as with most potential divorces, we owe it to ourselves to discuss the best- and worst-case outcomes in an attorney's office. If our future destiny is headed down a path of ugliness, we need to better understand what that ugliness could look like. It is now time to analyze the real-world ramifications associated with a geographical breakup of the United States of America.

Chapter 10: The Revolutionary Gamble of the Century

If you look at the map of the United States, there is all that red in the middle, places where Trump won. What the map doesn't show you is that I won the places that own two-thirds of America's gross domestic product. I won the places that are optimistic, diverse, dynamic, moving forward.

—Hillary Clinton

There exists the chance the US is already beyond the point of simple repair. America may once again be facing an 1860's set of revolutionary circumstances. We know how much life and treasure was lost in the *first* Civil War. What lessons can we learn from the past as we contemplate a *second* geographical breakup?

Today, both sides can make an argument for going it alone. At first glance, it seems like the "blue" states are in a stronger position to secede from the "red" states.[xcvii] Since the Great Recession, red and blue states have been traveling down divergent paths when it comes to income, education, and GDP growth.[xcviii] At our universities, blue states are typecast as hip, diverse, and cool, whereas red states are looked down upon as old, White, rural, and angry.

In progressive academic circles, there is much talk about which US states are *net givers* and which are *net takers*. That is, the difference between what an individual state pays into the federal government in taxes versus what it receives back from the feds in services. Using data from the Rockefeller Institute of Government, blue states like New York appear to be heavily subsidizing red states like Mississippi.[xcix] For every dollar New York pays into the federal government, they are only getting back eighty-six cents.[c] Conversely, for every dollar Mississippi pays, they are getting back double.[ci] Is it possible the so-called fiscally conservative red states would go broke first if the US were to splinter off into two countries?

As we contemplate the far-reaching concept of breaking up the US by geography, let's begin by addressing the flawed logic of people like Hillary Clinton and the NYT's Paul Krugman. These liberal talking heads are attempting to paint the picture that blue America is moving forward, while red is assumingly going backwards. If we take a closer look at the Rockefeller data, however, states that are home to America's military bases stand out when federal outflows are weighted against what the IRS brings in revenues.[cii] Military bases equate to a greater share of federal dollars. This reality explains why blue states with large military presences like Virginia, Maryland, and New Mexico score just as poorly on the Rockefeller rankings as red states like Kentucky and Louisiana.[ciii]

Secondly, states with higher levels of means-tested entitlements also skew the inflow/outflow data. Yes, it is true red states like Arkansas are drawing in significant federal dollars compared to other states.[civ] And yes, the statistics show New York and California appear to be getting a raw deal—especially with Trump's new tax plan.[cv] What is the inconvenient little secret in the *backwoods* red states?

A third of the population in states like Mississippi, Louisiana, and Arkansas are Black—a specific demographic that statistically takes in more dollars than it pays out in federal taxes.[cvi] What would the inflow/outflow ratios of lily-white blue states like Vermont and Connecticut look like if these demographics were reversed?[cvii] In fact, *why isn't there more diversity in Bernie Sanders' home state of Vermont?*

Lastly, life is also more complicated than just creating GDP. Take a guess at what states have the *fewest* military veterans per capita.

- Illinois
- Massachusetts
- California
- New Jersey
- New York

And which states have the *most* military veterans per capita?

- Alaska
- Montana
- Virginia
- Maine
- Oklahoma[cviii]

The *unenlightened* red-state citizens are more likely to fight and die for their country than their blue-state counterparts. And it is the red-state "deplorables" who are most likely to farm, build, and produce energy for both the blue and red states.[cix]

We can all agree that Silicon Valley is important to the success of America. But so are the Permian Basin and Great Plains regions. In addition, there is no guarantee that today's *blue states* would maintain their GDP advantage over a *future Red America,* should the two groups eventually go their own separate ways.

When the Civil War began, seven slave-holding states— South Carolina, Mississippi, Florida, Alabama, Georgia, Louisiana, and Texas—were the first to secede from the Union.[cx] They were later joined by North Carolina, Virginia, Arkansas, and Tennessee.[cxi] The issue of slavery was succinct, and big money was involved. Before the Civil War, the South was powerful because cotton was the biggest driver of the US economy.[cxii]

Of interest to us, the *GDP creators* in both regions *didn't* defect to the other side. They stayed put in their own backyards. This distinction brings us back to another important history lesson. What makes liberals like Clinton and Krugman so confident companies based in blue states today wouldn't pack up and move to a newly formed "Red America" should a second breakup occur?

The 1860's North and South were also unified in their respective causes. Today, there is no such unity in the Democrat Party. Half of the progressives are anti-capitalists. What makes the leftist elites so confident highly taxed venues like Manhattan and Silicon Valley aren't capable of becoming economic ghost towns tomorrow?

Abraham Lincoln is an icon revered for protecting the Union at nearly any cost. In what is an uncommon critique of Lincoln's decision to use war to prevent secession, Robert F. Hawes Jr., author of *One Nation Indivisible?: A Study of Secession and the Constitution,* argues that Lincoln would have been better off allowing the Southern states to go their own way without a fight.[cxiii] Hawes claims that by using the full force of the federal government, and even violating the US Constitution, Lincoln not only lost unnecessary life and treasure, but also the original intent of federalism and limited government.

Yes, Abraham Lincoln is nearly untouchable in his degree of wisdom, courage, and statesmanship, but was he wrong in not allowing the South to simply secede unencumbered? Should Abraham Lincoln have let the South simply wither away over time instead of initiating such a violent show of federal power?

Using Hawes's logic, there was a reasonable chance the 1860s South could have seceded in 1861, the North could have said farewell, and both sides could have pursued their own experiments without war. There is also a chance the South could have rejoined the Union after realizing it was wrong on the issue of slavery. Had this second course of action played out, America could have theoretically avoided its most costly war. In addition, the South could have handled the aftermath of slavery without big-brother-North pointing a gun to its head.[cxiv]

Why does this matter to us today? As Americans, we have been taught to believe the states are inseparable. Maybe this line of thinking was appropriate in 1861 when the US was more vulnerable to foreign adversaries, and maybe this logic still has merit today. But it is also plausible the fifty states no longer need each other in the same way they did in the nineteenth century. It is thus feasible a twenty-first-century United States could break off into two countries without the pretext of a bloody war.

Today, we hear about states like California and Texas seceding from the Union. Is it possible an individual state, or a group of states, could send a letter to the president and the Senate saying, "Let this correspondence serve as notice that California no longer considers itself a member state in the US. It is hereby our intention to negotiate a release from the US, its laws, and its Constitution.'"?

The US Constitution is silent on the idea of a state, or a group of states, seceding from the Union. Article IV, Section 3, Clause 1, only outlines the issue of adding additional states to the Union:

> New States may be admitted by the Congress into this Union; but no new State shall be formed or erected within the Jurisdiction of any other State; nor any State be formed by the junction of two or more States, or Parts of States, without the Consent of the Legislatures of the States concerned as well as Congress.[cxv]

Some states' rights advocates have argued that since state sovereignty predates the US Constitution, individual states have a natural right to leave any federal government deemed unjust. This talking point goes back to the founding and was carried into the Civil War. In 1869, however, the Supreme Court ruled in Texas vs. White that "unilateral secession is unconstitutional," while commenting that only *"revolution or consent of the states could lead to a successful secession."*[cxvi] More recently, the late conservative Supreme Court Justice Antonin Scalia said, "If there was any constitutional issue resolved by the Civil War, it is that no state has the right to secede."[cxvii]

Let's be clear about unilateral secession occurring in America. Barring an explosive set of revolutionary circumstances, this type of approach is not going to be the vehicle used to divide the US into two countries. The Supreme Court would never allow state(s) to secede unless the measure was constitutionally approved; that is, ratification by two-thirds majorities in the House and Senate, and thirty-eight state legislatures. Moreover, why would any blue state vote in favor of losing California's fifty-five electoral votes? The same goes for Texas and the other red states. In this sense, secession talk in California, Texas, and others is only conjecture.

In today's delicate balance of power, both blue and red states need every player on the team. If there is going to be a geographical divide, the plan is more likely to be hatched in the setting of a constitutional convention.

Under Article V, the founders scripted two ways to convene a convention. The first method is initiated in Congress by a two-thirds vote in both houses and then ratified by three-fourths of the state's legislatures. Of the twenty-seven amendments made to the Constitution, this amendment process has been used exclusively.

The second method in amending the Constitution was intended to give states constitutional authority without consent from the federal government. Under this latter Article V provision, a convention can be held when two-thirds of state legislatures call to order a constitutional meeting.[cxviii] Listed below is the verbiage that allows both methods:

Article V, US Constitution

"The Congress, whenever two thirds of both houses shall deem it necessary, shall propose amendments to this Constitution, or, on the application of the legislatures of two thirds of the several states, shall call a convention for proposing amendments, which, in either case, shall be valid to all intents and purposes, as part of this Constitution, when ratified by the legislatures of three fourths of the several states, or by conventions in three fourths thereof, as the one or the other mode of ratification may be proposed by the Congress; provided that no amendment which may be made prior to the year one thousand eight hundred and eight shall in any manner affect the first and fourth clauses in the ninth section of the first article; and that no state, without its consent, shall be deprived of its equal suffrage in the Senate."[cxix]

Is our way out of this bad marriage an invocation of an Article V convention? Some legal scholars have argued that an open-ended convention could blow up the entire Constitution. Let's again listen to Justice Scalia in 2014: "I certainly would not want a constitutional convention. Whoa! Who knows what would come out of it?"[cxx] It is certainly understandable a constitutional originalist like Scalia would have feared such an event could turn the entire document upside down. But much has changed since Justice Scalia died in 2016.

The US could be on the brink of a revolution. Trying to safeguard the Constitution when the walls of the house are collapsing is akin to grabbing onto a tree during a tornado. If we can't stop the barbarians from destroying national monuments, how long will it be before the anarchists start breaking down the windows of the National Archives Building?[cxxi]

Using the state-sponsored mechanism in Article V, it would take thirty-four states to convene a convention with participation from all fifty states. In this era of hyper-partisanship, it is reasonable to assume thirty-four state legislatures would authorize such a gathering. Let's not forget that blue states despise us as much as we dislike them.

Whether a constitutional convention is convened by the states or Congress, the goal would be about getting both sides together to either *save the marriage or to discuss moving on with the least amount of pain.*

Yes, this Article V talk carries significant risks. In an era where race relations are deteriorating and monuments are being knocked down, a convention would almost certainly expose old wounds. But short of an unexpected reconciliation between red/blue, Black/White, and Black/Brown/White what other choices do we have as a country?

There is a chance both sides could *divorce* and be much happier than they are today. Should there be a split in the US, it doesn't have to be violent. Look at our relationship with Canada. Canadians may be more progressive than Californians, yet despite our differences, they are a good neighbor and a great trading partner. Yes, Canada is fortunate to live next door to a neighbor who has the guns and fortitude to keep bad actors out of North America. But they are also a trusted ally.

A second divorce doesn't have to evolve into an ugly civil war. Both sides could structure a gradual breakup while maintaining mutual trade and commerce. Maybe one side will fail and be at the mercy of their former partner. Or maybe both sides will succeed and finally find the freedom to be who they want to be. Most importantly, *all of us* will be able to vote with our feet once the terms of the divorce are finalized.

Since the Article V verbiage is so vague, every source of tension would be fair game at a convention. There would be no filibusters, clotures, or gavels in such a setting. By today's standards, an invocation of an Article V Convention could be viewed as a no-holds-barred discussion where everything is on the table:

- How does America overcome the original sin of slavery?
- What are the pros and cons in dividing the United States of America?
- What would two Americas look like on paper?
- What would the national security ramifications associated with *two Americas* be?
- How would the national debt be accounted for?
- Would any re-created borders be "hard" or "soft?"

Under such an incredible set of revolutionary circumstances, the thought police would be placed on official notice. When lives, families, and careers are at stake, there will be little time for politically correct conversations. It would, in fact, be fascinating to watch an open convention play out on primetime television. Millions of Americans would be glued to their TVs, listening as both sides passionately debate the cultural, political, and philosophical issues of our era. An unfiltered convention would have the potential to drive voter passions to levels not witnessed since the Civil War.

Where do the liberals and traditionalists stand on Jefferson's Declaration of Independence? Would either side want to change this iconic document? If so, how? And what about the US Constitution—would either side dare alter the most transformative piece of paper in human history?

A constitutional convention would allow blue- and red-state representatives to present their twenty-first-century manifestos to the public. This type of event would carry real-world ramifications to every US citizen. Politicians on both sides would speak extensively in back rooms about future alliances, redrawn borders, strategic advantages/disadvantages, federalism, and money. It is even possible Canada and Mexico could join the discussion(s.)

Should a convention lead to the discussion of breaking up the country, the list of negotiating points would be initially endless. Both sides would seek to reshape "two new Americas" to align with their views of philosophy, morality, and politics. While *red* Americans would likely prioritize limited government, constitutional originalism, and Judeo-Christian values, what would *blue* Americans prioritize? In the spirit of universalism, would a newly created Blue America accept every global applicant for immediate citizenship? If Red America were to tighten the requirements associated with voting and citizenship, would the new Blue America accept all transfer-requests with no strings attached?

Further, if one is a red-state American living in a newly formed Blue America, what would their options be? Could they still live in a blue state and pay taxes into a newly formed Red

America? If a blue-state voter ended up residing in a red state, would their right to vote apply to Red America, Blue America, or both? Yes, there would be certain societal covenants that newly created Blue and Red Americas may agree on. Both would likely maintain their obligations of paying into Social Security and Medicare. But what about currency?

During the Civil War, the Confederacy printed the "Greyback," but the paper money was never backed by anything more than a promise of victory over the North.[cxxii] After the war was over, the Confederate currency was worthless. How would both sides resolve the issue of money today? And beyond the significant question of debt and currency, there are other complex negotiating dilemmas like national defense, citizenship rights, property rights, and treaty obligations.

Is it possible the revolutionary sparks flying from a courtroom-like battle could have the potential to wake up those apathetic Americans sitting on the sidelines? First- and second-generation Brown Americans, for example, would come to understand there is more to American-style liberty than taking easy multiple-choice exams to gain citizenship. Would Latinos and Asians choose open borders, free stuff, and high taxes, or would they pick an America that values traditional definitions of gender, an entrepreneurial business environment, and limited government?

Would Black Americans be suspicious of the do-gooder Whites and their big bag of freebies? Could a geographical split have the power of doing what Lincoln couldn't do 150 years ago—unite Whites and Blacks with shared values instead of forced assimilation? Or would most Blacks leave the newly formed Red America fearing limited government, personal accountability, and strong families are a backdoor way of legalizing *systematic racism*?

What about Generations Y and Z? A constitutional convention would be a lot more exciting for younger

Americans than listening to boring history professors. Would younger Americans pick open genders and free stuff over the traditional triage of God, family, and country? Maybe. But either way, they would live to witness one of the biggest social science experiments in the history of mankind. In the end, the millennials may finally discover the answers to today's great divide:

• Is human nature malleable enough to one day guarantee equal outcomes?
• Which political ideology leads to greater satisfaction and purpose in life—nanny-state governance policed by central planners or individual liberty protected by guns?
• Are traditional parents and grandparents unenlightened stooges for the bourgeoisie, or are older Whites the last line of defense against tyranny and authoritarian rule?

Geographically, ninety-six percent of the country votes Republican.[cxxiii] Democrats monopolize coastal regions, university towns, and urban areas. If a constitutional convention led to the radical notion of breaking up the country by region, states as we know them today would likely be redrawn with name changes. It is easy to say, "Give the Democrats the East and West Coasts, and we'll take the rest." But should such a split occur, states like California and New York could splinter inside and outside their present-day borders. If one were to drive forty minutes beyond downtown LA and New York City, there are millions of Americans who wouldn't want anything to do with their big-city cousins once any divorce went public.

Should an Article V Convention result in a land split, a newly rejuvenated Red America could repurpose Republican apathy and dysfunction into a future foundation of hope, optimism, and purpose. This type of *redo* would allow the traditionalist to put their *new United States* on solid footing for future generations. Young and old would become united by the kinship that comes with going into battle as one. Like-minded Blacks and Whites would say goodbye to Uncle Tom and the ghosts of slavery. Latinos and Asians would no longer be walking in the limbo land of divided Whites. And the days of using labels like African American, Hispanic American, and Muslim American would officially end. Instead of feeling guilty and divided, a new Red America would be uplifted by big ideas and freed from the tyranny of political correctness.

As for our ex-partners, maybe they can finally find their real-world utopia without having us standing in their way. In what could become the ultimate game of revolutionary poker, blue could finally move beyond America's history of racism, privilege, and inequality and make everything right with the various victim classes. Without Republican obstruction, a new Blue America could easily implement free college, abolish the use of fossil fuels, grant reparations to Blacks, and open their borders to every global refugee.

Is it possible that having a more public and radical discussion in a raucous convention environment could flush out the leftist radicals in the same way McCarthy was exposed in the 1950s? Maybe. But it is more likely that once the door of an Article V Convention is opened, there will be no turning back. In the end, an open convention could be judged in the context of history as the first formalized step of a *third* American divorce.[2]

---

[2] For reference, the author suggests the Revolutionary War was Divorce #1, and the US Civil War was Divorce #2.

There are, of course, no guarantees an open Article V Convention would happen in today's cutthroat era of politics—just as there is a chance an actual convention could make things even worse than they already are today. What happens if our convention idea blows up into a frenzy and nothing gets resolved? What is the backup plan should an Article V Convention never occur? The next step in our process is to take a walk down the hypothetical road of our first ugly divorce.

Donald Trump's bellicosity may not be a democratic accident. Trump would have never been elected to the presidency if we were living in a stable democracy. In this sense, it may simply be too late for a peaceful parting of ways. Donald Trump, whether intended or not, has forever changed the rules of engagement. Politically, President Trump is the belligerent uncle who crashed the passive-aggressive family party where tension was always lingering behind the small talk and fake smiles. He is sowing chaos and initiating unpleasant conversations in every corner of the room. And like the family of the crazy uncle, things may never be the same once the Donald Trump party ends.

What happens to our mass-movement plan if Trump loses in 2020? Obviously, the other side would be incredibly happy. But what would *we* do? And what happens if Trump wins? Should we give an active president a revolutionary handbook that dares to break up the union of the United States of America?

Chapter 11: The Bad Divorce with Trump Out

Pick the target, freeze it, personalize it, and polarize it. Cut off the support network and isolate the target from sympathy.

—*Saul Alinsky*

What do we mean when we say, a "bad divorce?" Let's expand on this concept further for very good reason. This type of strategy would be used when all else fails and one or both sides come to hate the *incompetence, hypocrisy, and injustice* of their political adversary. A traditionalist-led mass movement would develop when today's apathy and displeasure escalated into widespread anger and hatred of the progressive intellectuals, artists, and politicians. Under such a scenario, the traditionalist would come to prioritize *retribution* and *justice* over personal safety and comfort.

In a revolutionary environment, life as we know it today would probably be turned upside down. The list of unintended consequences would be limitless. As with the Revolutionary and Civil War(s), Americans would pick sides and mass migrations of millions of human beings could occur. Martial law could be enacted, bank accounts could be seized, and food shortages may occur. The writ of habeas corpus could be suspended, and civil liberties would be in jeopardy. Outside of

137

the US, a power vacuum could jeopardize the lives of millions of human beings. And assuming "America" re-emerges from such internal strife, a revolution could set the country back in the context of years and not months.

We are now moving closer into the world of ugly and unpredictable. Let's begin this process by formally introducing two twentieth-century historians who wrote extensively about mass-movement and revolutionary theory. The late historian Crane Brinton analyzed the conditions associated with the British Revolution, the American Revolution, the French Revolution, and the Russian Revolution. Brinton posited all four revolutions saw an upward path of economic growth prior to the revolutionary outbreaks; an angst among the downtrodden and the middle and upper classes of society; inept governance and unfair taxation; a transfer of allegiance from the intellectual classes; and division between the old ruling classes of society.[cxxiv] Brinton hypothesized revolutions "must be made respectable and must touch the soul."[cxxv] He wrote the four major revolutions "clearly were not born in societies economically retrograde." On the contrary, they took place in societies that were on the rise before an economic downturn occurred.

Brinton:

The years preceding the outbreak of revolution witnessed unusually serious economic, or at least financial, difficulties of a special kind...and that revolutions often come during economic depressions, which follow on periods of generally rising standards of living."[cxxvi]

Eric Hoffer wrote extensively on the psychology of mass movements after World War II and noted the "new poor" would often be reliable foot soldiers in a revolution.[cxxvii] Like Brinton, Hoffer theorized mass movements could be triggered by people who had found societal status and then lost it.[cxxviii] He believed such an event is more likely when the military classes of society are demoralized.[cxxix] In terms of leadership, he maintained the revolutionary leader does not "create the conditions which make the rise of a movement possible," but "once the stage is set, the presence of an outstanding leader is indispensable. Without him, there will be no movement."[cxxx] Both Brinton and Hoffer believed a successful mass movement required a strong element of hope in conjunction with a clearly defined "evil" or "devil."[cxxxi] [cxxxii]

We are not going to assume Brinton and Hoffer had the foresight to predict a twenty-first-century American mass movement. Even Brinton acknowledged, "Revolutions are more remarkable for their differences."[cxxxiii] Though, if we believe human nature is geared to a predictable arc of power and regeneration, these men may offer some clues to our own path forward.

When Americans think of revolutions, they envision the proletariat (working classes) rising and overthrowing the bourgeoisie (wealthy elites). This is probably due to the overwhelming Marxist bias found at Western universities. But if we look back into history, our first divorce had nothing to do with class envy. The Founding Fathers were not poor and destitute when the Revolutionary War broke out. Nearly all of those men came from the highest orders of society, and they risked their lives to pursue the freedoms we enjoy today.[cxxxiv]

Contrary to Marxist logic, a twenty-first-century American mass movement can occur when the wealthy, the skilled working classes, and the military classes align in *hating* the ruling elites. Moving forward, we will refer to this group as the Haves, Doers, and Warriors.[cxxxv] The "Haves" are the millionaires and billionaires who possess the power to fund politicians and mass movements. Amazingly, this group today

J. N. Welch

is nearly split 50/50 between the Democrats and Republicans.[cxxxvi] The "Doers" are the highly skilled men and women in the middle who keep the country running on a day-to-day basis. Without the Doers, we wouldn't have engineers, nurses, doctors, programmers, farmers, factory workers, scientists, builders, mechanics, miners, and the many other highly skilled professions that take years of training to master. The "Warriors" are our military and law enforcement stewards. There is a balance in all these societal relationships, and the primary goal of the Marxist is to sow discord between each group in a manner that results in class struggle and eventual revolution against the Haves.

Saul Alinsky referred to two additional groups who may become relevant to our discussion: the "Have-Nots" and the "Have-a-Little, Want Mores."[cxxxvii] Today, these Americans can be defined as the young, unskilled, and non-Whites who are most likely to buy into the progressive notion the system is rigged, and the only way "out" is to vote against Republicans. As we discussed previously, there is plenty of evidence to support the belief the GOP is out of touch. In a global economy, big money can be made by the innovative classes of society. Conversely, unskilled workers always seem to be subservient to forces beyond their control. The Marxists' aim is to keep this latter group hopeless, perpetually marginalized, and on standby for a revolution. *Our* revolutionary goal will be to create a new movement that has a strong message of hope backed by policies that can improve family structures, schools, and the employee/employer compact.

While many Republicans find horror in a progressive presidency, I see a Trump exit as a civil reboot opportunity. The mass-movement problem with Donald Trump is that half of the electorate despises him. Throughout his presidency, Trump has been bailing water out of the *Titanic* with a five-gallon bucket. While an insider president could incite the proper conditions required for a future widespread mass movement, Trump would still be an insider who would likely

140

be held responsible for any civil disobedience that occurred under his watch. In the context of a revolutionary environment, Trump could simply be more impactful from the outside than from the inside.

Let's begin by taking a closer look at a Trump departure in 2020, 2024, or otherwise. When Donald Trump vacates the presidency, there will likely be an initial honeymoon period with the Democrats, the media, and Hollywood. There would be a great sense of satisfaction in toppling the "dictator." On the traditionalist side, however, a Trump exit would lead to a temporary void, and his supporters would feel like they pushed all their chips in and lost. But this mindset would be a mistake. Should Trump suddenly depart the stage, the GOP would meekly jump back onto the scene and declare a return to civility and orderly governance, and we would be right back to having a Romney or Bush.

Instead of pursuing an aggressive mass-movement mentality, traditionalists would instead face guilt from the Democrats *and* from the GOP for previously supporting Trump with such zeal. I can already hear the Republican establishment: "Americans need to heal and find a way back to civility and bipartisanship. We need to unite our country and start working together again as one people."

Once Trump is out of the picture as a sitting president, there may be a significant opportunity for a counterinsurgency-like mass movement. Using a coordinated effort, the new *traditional radicals* would avoid following the same path Nancy Pelosi and Chuck Schumer took when Trump won in 2016. Forget the endless impeachment hearings. Instead, we should consider the strategic concept of going into a "retrenchment" mode. What does this concept mean? A retrenchment would imply traditional voters would walk away from the national GOP once Trump exits the White House. And they would return once they repurposed themselves into a unified movement that has the majority power, and conviction, to take the fight directly to their fascist foe.

I am suggesting, once Trump is gone, a traditional-led movement should consider using the "*new political platform*" and "*new political party*" rebranding idea that we discussed as *the good divorce* option. We would allow the Democrats to temporarily run the national government in a nearly unencumbered manner while we worked underground to build a new and lasting movement. This type of grassroots declaration would represent an astounding moment in American politics. It would be the first time in the US that the people, and *not* the elites, completely overhauled a political party from the ground up.

Previous GOP voters would use a presidential defeat as an opportunity to retrench, rebuild, and allow the other side to take real ownership of their misguided views on human nature, economics, and morality. Although the media would never say so, the Democrats have bigger problems than the Republicans do. Moderate Democrats are getting squeezed hard by the extreme elements of their party. The Bill Clinton Democrats are close to becoming dinosaurs in this new era of Tlaibs and AOCs. Why not expose the Democrats' deep dysfunction for all to see while we rebuild and learn how to become an organized resistance movement from the outside looking in?

Under such a retrenchment plan, any remaining Republicans in D.C. would join the resistance movement or risk being replaced by it. Using a coordinated plan that would essentially manipulate the American democracy, traditional radicals would consider sitting out the 2022 midterm congressional elections. Traditional voters would still vote to keep Republicans in state and local offices—this is not where the true cancer lies. Republican states and, hopefully, the Supreme Court may be helpful advocates once the revolutionary tensions rise to a mass-movement level. But assuming the conditions were right, we would allow the

Democrats to own the federal government without having any Republicans standing in the crossfire. Instead of trying to be *bipartisan*, the job of any holdover congressional Republicans would be to expose hypocrisy with an insiders view.

Now, I admit the strategy of allowing the Democrats unfettered control of the federal government can be interpreted as self-inflicted nihilism. This type of approach could result in:

- Nationalized health care being established in the US.
- Democrats packing the courts with leftist ideologues.
- Borders opening to millions of undocumented immigrants.
- The US military budget being gutted.

It would obviously be gut-check time should any such partisan overreach occur. But what better alternative do we have in our current set of circumstances? We have been bleeding a slow death for decades. As Donald Trump would say, "What else do we have to lose?" Look at what happened after the iconic Reagan left office—what did we get? George Bush Sr. and George Bush Jr. True, we got some good judges and bureaucrats from the father and son presidencies, but neither were able turn a leftist tide that began in the 1960s, stalled in the 1980s, and returned in full force under Bush Jr.

Can we honestly say having Bush and Bush instead of Dukakis and Gore would have made any type of material difference to our present-day problems? In fact, *we may have been better off without either of those men as presidents.* We may have been able to flush out the progressive insanity sooner had these guys—especially the son—never walked onto the stage.

I admit, a Bernie Sanders-like presidency would be a dream come true to the agitation-minded traditionalist. Sanders is a true believer who, if given the opportunity, couldn't run a lemonade stand. What is the biggest threat to a Marxist? Their kryptonite occurs when they are forced to move from revolutionary rhetoric to real-world decision making. If one wishes to expose the Marxist revolutionary, cut off a piece of California, Oregon, and Washington and let the do-gooders open their new country to millions of freeloaders. Or let them raise their corporate tax rate to 90 percent and watch Silicon Valley head for the exits.

Applying this logic to today, Trump should allow lawless anarchists, BLM, and progressive do-gooders in Democrat-run cities full autonomy to govern themselves. Trust me—the millennials in these *utopias* will get more of an education in four months than they did in four years at Harvard.

A Joe Biden-like presidency complicates our ability to show contrast between two forces of *light and darkness*. The problem for the traditionalist is he or she loses ground every time an establishment figurehead is elected to the presidency. The newly elected Democrat, or even Republican, promises to restore unity and bipartisanship. What does this mean to us? It means we are about to get drawn into another four years of lost mass-movement opportunities. The debt, dysfunction, and the *intellectual cancer* in our schools and culture will continue. Having someone like Joe Biden in the White House means the college professors and their pop culture allies would get four more years of uninterrupted time to pollute millions of additional minds.

And politically, the country would likely be put into the situation where the AOCs are pushing Biden hard and the establishment Republicans are fighting back against the leftist crazies. Meanwhile, *President Joe Biden* ends up standing above the fray as a "common sense" president.

A Biden presidency *doesn't* mean we would wait four more years to go underground. We would, however, be smarter in our approach of letting the Democrats control the federal government. Maybe we would stay home on Election Day in 2022 but come back in 2024. Or maybe we would sit out both or neither. But we would be *patient* and *flexible* in allowing overreach to occur.

Most importantly, we would be disciplined enough to wait for Crane Brinton's smoke signals: *"Angst among the downtrodden and the middle and upper classes of society; inept governance and unfair taxation; a transfer of allegiance from the intellectual classes; and division between the old ruling classes of society."*[cxxxviii]

A Trump exit could represent a tremendous opportunity to turn pain and anger into the first steps of a real mass movement. We messed up in letting things get this far. We exploded the debt and slowly allowed the radicals in academia to take over traditional culture. Isn't it our turn to demand a new movement that can expose and defeat the stealthy oppressors who have moved into our homes, places of worship, and businesses?

Such a plan would include the following elements:

- Abandoning and/or overhauling of the Republican Party and platform.
- Manipulating the democratic process in the short run to intentionally allow national Democrats the ability to pass legislation with little to no Republican encumbrance.
- Going underground to develop a bold, twenty-first-century political platform.
- Allowing moderate Democrats and independents a voice at the new table.

- Finding national leaders willing to speak beyond political correctness and establishment-minded politics.
- Planting mass-movement seeds within the US military.
- Recruiting Browns, Blacks, and females to become future resistance leaders.
- Encouraging individual states to initiate "civil disobedience" campaigns against the federal government.
- Creating a level of *anger and discontent* that has the potential to lead to widespread civil unrest.

A Democratic president, in conjunction with a Democrat-led House and Senate, would represent an ideal time for traditionalists to reorganize. Our mass-movement plan would further seek to:

- Turn a Trump loss into an opportunity to discard the stale Republican Party and start with a fresh set of ideas and players.
- Pit establishment Democrats against the Bernie Sanders Democrats.
- Allow the radical left nearly complete autonomy to find their utopia.
- Develop an "agitation plan" that would seek to drive the new progressive custodians of American society crazy.

What is an "agitation plan?" In a revolutionary context, an *agitation* phase would refer to that defining moment when one side decides to openly fight back against the ruling elites using asymmetrical tactics. To us, the agitation stage would begin once Republican voters walk away from the establishment and demand new players and a new playbook. If Hoffer and

Brinton are correct, the goal of an agitation period is to antagonize the other side until their *"prevailing order is discredited."*[cxxxix] In layman's terms, this would mean we would help the Democrats self-destruct to where they were hated by most of the electorate.

As we consider life beyond Trump, let's begin by putting some perspective into the marriage. Whether today or in the future, we can't predict how many traditional Americans would have the stomach to let the Democrats run the country in a nearly arbitrary fashion. Nor can we predict what trigger points could pull more Blacks, Browns, and females away from the power of identity politics. Honestly, we may have to wait a long while before a serious mass movement takes root. Our cat-and-mouse game could take years instead of months.

As the people of action, the Doers, Haves, and Warriors have a natural inclination to dismiss bureaucrats, artists, and academics as *nerds on a playground.* We ask ourselves, "How can they be so weird?" But maybe we should take a closer look at our own arrogance. We have most of the guns and money, yet we are close to losing the biggest fight of the twenty-first century. *The nerds* have nearly won over our kids, the media, and pop culture without firing a shot. What is wrong in borrowing parts of their agitation playbook and having a little fun doing so? Let's listen to Alinsky:

> Ridicule is man's most impotent weapon. A good tactic is one your people will enjoy. If you're not having a ball doing it, there is something very wrong with the tactic.[cxl]

Barring a *contested* election due to voting irregularities, the traditional radicals wouldn't want to come out guns-a-blazing after a Trump loss. Yes, time is running out in turning the tables on the leftists and Marxists. And yes, there is nothing funny about the crazies who are close to overturning a global order. But if we don't find the proper blend of brevity, patience, and persistence this time around, we will end up following the same marginalized route of the Tea Party.

Let's find perspective in these extraordinary times. Let's provoke, antagonize, and agitate the other side without taking ourselves so damn seriously. And then, let's go back to Saul Alinsky for the most important element of an agitation mass-movement strategy:

> For example, since the Haves publicly pose as the custodians of responsibility, morality, law, and justice (which are frequently strangers to each other), they can be constantly pushed to live up to their own book of morality and regulations. No organization, including organized religion, can live up to the letter of its own book. You can club them to death with their "book" of rules and regulations.[cxli]

Once the traditionalist truly understands he or she has become the distressed minority, the new ruling elites would be forced to "live up to their own playbook of morality and regulations."[cxlii] What would their priorities be once they become the official stewards of "responsibility, morality, law, and justice?" Their list would probably look something like this:

- wealth redistribution
- reparation for Blacks
- defunding law enforcement
- a Green New Deal
- nationalized health care

- cutting back on military spending
- climate change
- open borders
- gender equality and pay
- free college for all.

It doesn't take a Saul Alinsky to see how much fun we could have "clubbing them to death" with their own book of rules.[cxliii] This would mean red states would pick constant fights with the federal government, traditional voters would antagonize progressive elites, and consumers would make companies pay a price for lying in bed with leftist fanatics. Under such an agitation strategy, the traditionalist radicals would seek to hold every leftist influencer a hundred percent accountable to their Democrat Socialist playbook.

Look at how effective today's leftists are in bullying companies to achieve political means. As outside agitators, we would turn the tables and learn how to exploit inconsistencies and hypocrisies to our mass-movement advantage. Just like us, the Democrats are unprincipled. Today's progressive elites are not living in 1,200-square-foot bungalows in low-income areas; they are more likely to own three mansions and have a carbon footprint the size of some small towns. How did Al Gore make $200 million dollars after he left D.C.?[cxliv] How did Chelsea Clinton's net worth become over ten million dollars?[cxlv] If Elizabeth Warren supports public schools so much, why did her son attend an elite private school?[cxlvi] And how did Hunter Biden make millions of dollars in the Ukrainian natural gas industry?[cxlvii] What does Hunter Biden know about natural gas exploration?

Should the timing be right, traditional agitators would also consider inciting "illegal" behavior to provoke the ruling classes to either stand down or punish the revolutionaries for *their improper* behavior. Here's Brinton again:

> In each revolution there is a point, or
> several points, where constituted authority is
> challenged by the illegal acts of the
> revolutionists. In such instances, the routine
> response of any authority is to have recourse
> to force, police, or military.[cxlviii]

We're not asking traditional radicals to be lawless
thugs. We're not looters. We are friends of law enforcement
and the military. We're not going to put our friends and allies
in awkward situations. We would instead be calculated and
smart in how we break laws, customs, and PC norms. If
these types of mass-movement tactics are done well, the "new
custodians" of society would find themselves having to walk
the fine line of enforcing their utopian playbooks with
apprehension from law enforcement and the military. In what
would essentially become a delicate game of cat-and-mouse,
the traditionalist would seek to agitate the do-gooder elites into
the unenviable position of having to use an unsympathetic
group of Warriors to stop the *illegal* behavior of the Haves and
Doers. Then we would seek to exploit any overreactions or
underreactions to our advantage.

As an organized resistance movement, the traditionalist
would aspire to create a level of hatred that would cause
everyday people to despise the hypocrisy and double standards
of the leftist intelligentsia. We would coordinate police
boycotts in radical blue cities and ask traditionalist Haves to
provide financial assistance to their Warrior allies during any
such standoffs. If someone like Alexandria Ocasio-Cortez
sought to disband the police, *we* would begin by asking our
police friends to *stay home sick* in her congressional district of
the Bronx and Queens.[3]

The Haves, Doers, and Warriors do not have the structural
handicaps the Have-Nots had in the 1960s. Traditionalist
agitators could be very creative in how they forced the leftist

elites to live up to their own rules. From an organizational standpoint, the Haves, Doers, and Warriors could accomplish in five years what took Saul Alinsky fifty years to do.

What is the end goal with a *bad divorce* strategy?

- To create a level of civil unrest that can expose and defeat the intellectual contagion of our era.
- *To win today's ideological battle—on our terms.*
- To build a new and repurposed country, unified beyond race and ethnic origin.
- To show the world Americans will use revolutionary tactics to defeat tyranny on its own soil.

Is this strategy wrought with unintended consequences? Of course. No one can predict with precise detail how a real divorce would play out between two people, let alone 300 million. Keeping this type of movement unified would also require great timing and the eventual emergence of a great leader.

I acknowledge it might make sense to simply throw in the towel after a Trump loss. But is this who *we* are? Assuming the right set of mass-movement buttons get pushed, there are millions of patriots willing to risk personal comfort to get their

---

3 Alexandria Ocasio-Cortez congressional coverage is District 14, which includes parts of the Bronx and Queens: Astoria, College Point, Corona, North Corona, East Elmhurst, Elmhurst, Jackson Heights, Sunnyside, and Woodside in Queens. Pelham Gardens, City Island, Country Club, Van Nest, Morris Park, Parkchester, Pelham Bay, Schuylerville, Allerton, and Throggs Neck in the Bronx.

country back into shape. Our strategy would seek to expose the fallacies of the college professors, the media, and Hollywood through tactics of public exposure, personal humiliation, and strategic lawlessness. At the same time, we'd be working underground and around the clock to build a powerful and lasting movement that could eventually restore sanity and purpose back into the American spirit.

We saw how quickly life can change with the coronavirus outbreak of 2020. If Hoffer and Brinton are correct, all it would take is the proper combination of agitation, hypocrisy, and anger, and the table could be quickly set to allow more old-school Democrats, Blacks, Latinos, Asians, and Jews time to rethink their political loyalties.

Is it possible an ex-president Trump could lead the agitation movement from the outside? Yes, but it is also time for us to get into the game. Today, we're reluctant to say we support Trump in public. We are afraid to wear the red hats. We attend sporting events where athletes kneel and play *two American* national anthems. We also stand down as the namesakes of heroes from the past are knocked down by fanatics. How can any civilization disregard its entire past without eventually sabotaging its own future? At what point will it be time to make a stand with courage, conviction, and an Alinsky level of organization?

One may then ask, what happens to our mass movement if Donald Trump wins? If the president is reelected, there would be unimaginable grief on the progressive side. The first four years of Trump required personal therapy and never-ending impeachment hearings for them. A second term could push the other side past grief to anger and retribution. It's entertaining to watch the *academics* fact-check Trump on all his "lies." The smart people still haven't figured out that Trump's appeal is mostly emotional. In a sense, Trump represents the most promising path in linking a once-glorious past to a repurposed future.

Donald Trump is a revolutionary leader. This explains why he is allowed so much latitude by his followers. His voters are looking at *the big picture*; they don't care about all his "lies" and grandstanding. In their heart of hearts, Trump's supporters simply wanted a sympathetic ally who could take the fight directly to the enemy.

If Donald Trump *does* manage to stay in the game, why not give him a playbook with mass-movement implications? Think about another four years of revolutionary trigger points in a 2020-24 Trump presidency. What will happen if Trump wins and gets *more* Supreme Court appointees? And what would happen if this sequence of events led to a Democrat-controlled House and Senate, increasing the number of Supreme Court justices from nine to fifteen? What happens if Trump only gets 5-10 percent of Black support in a second term, and Blacks continue to up the ante with rioting, kneeling, and looting? What would happen to our marriage if the federal government doesn't have enough creditworthiness to continue throwing around trillions of dollars? Would a sitting president try to initiate a state-sponsored Article V Convention? Would Trump brazenly violate the US Constitution to agitate blue states into unilateral secession talks?

Most of all, however, would Donald Trump ask the US military to be on standby for the possibility of an ugly divorce?

Chapter 12: The Bad Divorce with Trump In

The quality of the ideas seems to play a minor role in mass movement leadership. What counts is the arrogant gesture, the complete disregard of the opinions of others, the singlehanded defiance of the world.

—*Eric Hoffer*

While a *third* American revolution may seem unlikely, the underlying fault lines may already be in place:

- Two of the last four presidents have been impeached.
- There exists a political divide potentially greater than that of the Civil War.
- The left is moving toward Marxism, and the right is moving to the strongman.
- There is a massive accumulation of national debt.
- Americans are witnessing an emerging and aggressive China.
- Unresolved racial tensions are rearing their ugly head again.

- Global economic and political uncertainties are arising.

I'm not asking anyone do anything crazy right now. We can enjoy life with perspective. But should Donald Trump win a second term, there may be an opportunity that might never exist again in our lifetimes.

If reelected, Trump should immediately announce the Republican Party will be radically overhauled into an official *Trump doctrine*. A post-2020 Trump would want to make the three pocketbook issues of wages, pensions, and health insurance a legislative priority. And assuming a new traditional platform follows the discarded Republican playbook, Asian and Latino Americans should promptly receive their long-awaited welcome packages in the form of a new immigration policy.

In today's political climate, another four years of Trump would seem like an eternity to his haters. As a sitting president, Trump could control the divorce strings like a puppet master. A second-term Trump presidency would seek to make additional friends before declaring war on his enemies. When the timing was right, Trump would agitate the leftist radicals into overplaying their hands as lawless anarchists. And assuming Blacks continue to project the dysfunction in their urban communities onto the police and the entire American founding, Trump could easily incite racial tensions further than they are today—all while increasing his support with moderate Whites and Browns.

Trump's ultimate second-term decision may be to contemplate the opposite of what Lincoln had to think about in the 1860s. Rather than protecting the Union at any cost, Donald Trump could become the first American president to actively consider the idea of breaking up the United States by geography.

In a revolutionary environment, Donald Trump should consider using the bully pulpit of the presidency to prepare, agitate, and move the United States toward the future path of becoming two countries. And this fight should begin where our marital fault lines began—at our universities.

Our biggest enemies today are the social science and humanities professors who have the power to indoctrinate entire generations of Americans with a Marxist poison pill. If we want to defeat *our enemy*, Trump should declare war on academia. He should make his intentions known not as a commencement speaker, but as an outside agitator who knocks down doors. In this era of intellectual smoke and mirrors, Trump should consider using the presidency to finally expose the devil in our divorce story.

Hindsight taught us that establishment Republican and Tea Party tactics presented little threat to the college professors. Here's how a group of older Whites picketing outside a university would play out in a typical college classroom:

Professor:

All of us have First Amendment rights to protest in the United States. There is a lot of division in America these days. How many of you saw the protesters outside when you were walking to class? Yes, I saw them too. How many of the protesters looked like you? This is a big problem. There is a generational gap between you and them. Many of those folks are angry at you and me, but they came from an era when it was okay for women to be subservient to their husbands. They came from a period when it was acceptable to force Black people to the back of buses. And in their day, if you were born gay, you were out of luck. You would be stuck in the closet without ever being able to realize your true worth and potential as a human being. They have a right to protest, but so do you! Do we want to return to a point in time when being born Brown, Black, female, or LGBTQ—*anything* other than White and male—relegated you to second-class citizenry? This is certainly not the America I want to go back to.

This type of conventional strategy by older, establishment-minded Whites is not remotely adequate in beating the college professors at their own game. Fortunately for us, however, Donald Trump does not use an establishment playbook.

There is a chance a Trump victory could put the professors on their heels with the pure power of Trump's personality and Twitter. Think about the president declaring universities should be held financially responsible if a graduate can't find a job that justifies the cost of college. Think about Trump ridiculing some of the ludicrous classes that are being taught at our finest colleges: History of Surfing, Lady Gaga and the Sociology of Fame, and Tree Climbing.[cxlix] And yes, think about Trump holding massive rallies outside of Harvard and Yale, attacking the most sacred of all college professor sacraments—academic freedom.

Crane Brinton discussed the role of intellectuals in a revolutionary context:

> We may say that in a society markedly unstable there seem to be absolutely more intellectuals... bitterly attacking existing institutions and desirous of a considerable alteration of society, business, and government... we may compare intellectuals of this sort to

> white corpuscles, guardians of the blood stream;
> but there can be an excess of white corpuscles,
> and when this happens, you have a pathological
> condition.[cl]

America has a pathological condition that originated inside its universities. Until we realize where the mass-movement fight needs to begin, the Republican commentators in the media are simply grabbing at *ghosts*. Today, academic freedom has metastasized into academic tyranny. It doesn't help that twenty-first-century "intellectuals" belong to unions. Unions, by their very nature, incentivize solidarity and uniformity. This dynamic may explain why so few physical science academics are willing to call out their crazy colleagues in the social science departments.

Donald Trump, Republican governors, and like-minded college administrators should all reign in the monopoly of thought masquerading as an education. In addition, a second-term Trump could inspire thousands of students to become classroom agitators. If we think about it, now is a great time to be a *traditional radical* in a college environment. Confidence in life doesn't always come from hanging out with the majority crowd. True confidence comes from being around adversity and, more importantly, embracing it. In a mass-movement environment, I am asking traditional-minded college students to fully maximize the opportunity that comes with being a *minority* attending university. Yes, focus on your GPA, but don't miss the life lessons and friendships that coincide with forming a resistance movement with other like-minded students. If college professors are the true source of today's tensions, why not "*club them over the head*" with their own rulebooks?[cli]

As an adult college student, I would ask social science professors how they reconciled their Marxist beliefs to six-figure salaries. Or I would ask them why they would use any type of privately developed medicine if they believed in a government-run system. Or why would they drive gas-burning cars if fossil fuels are ruining the planet. When they asked me follow-up questions, I would sometimes respond with a smile, "I'm not sure—don't you think I'm too *privileged* to adequately answer such questions without bias?"

I understand it's difficult for a nineteen-year-old college student to use this tone in a classroom. Professors are confident in their theoretical castles, and they may grade unfairly. In all honesty, it took me years to learn how to ask these questions with brevity, humor, and respect without coming across as disruptive or angry. In this sense, it may be easier for traditional students to become social media agitators from the outside. Nowadays, students can use their laptops to post rogue professor rants on YouTube. Or they can choose to expose and embarrass biased professors on RateMyProfessor.com. Today's traditionalist students could make life very uncomfortable for a professor without ever uttering one word in a classroom.

Under the right set of circumstances, professors could be forced to "walk on eggshells" every time they step into their classrooms—especially male professors. Depending on how far college agitators want to take things, every progressive male in power can easily be "Kavanaughed."[clii] Did a male college professor ever use his position to have sex with a female student? Did he ever wear blackface to a frat party? What about controversial social media posts and texts from high school or college—were there any signs of male toxicity, xenophobia, or misogyny before the he reached his PhD status?

With or without Trump, traditionalist radicals should make life hell on the universities. If the battle lines begin there, why would any Republican (or Democrat) billionaire donate money to their alma maters? For what—to get their names engraved on a new monument that could easily be torn down by a future generation of radicalized students? Why not instead fund a movement that seeks to expose the anti-American lunacy that originates on college campuses?

Should younger Americans, and their parents, begin to question the trillion-dollar student debt racket in greater numbers, there also exists the possibility the Marxist professors could be squeezed out by the economics they so despise. Fewer students attending college in the soft majors would diminish the power of universities. Just as it is possible a new employer/employee partnership could diminish the power of academia.

Why don't more companies recruit smart and motivated *high-school seniors*? The military has been using this approach for decades. More recently, Tesla's Elon Musk suggested he values "exceptional ability" over a college degree.[cliii] If the universities continue to protect their leftist crusaders with impunity, why not bypass the conventional wisdom of college altogether? Moreover, this new arrangement could be a win-win for both employees and employers. Instead of wasting time to pursue a useless college degree, high school graduates could avoid student debt loans, move to exciting cities, and pick up four years of income *without all the debt*. In addition, companies could get ahead of the professors by prioritizing common sense and real-world application over theoretical classroom nonsense.

A second-term Trump would also seek to maintain a list of those colleges that continued to prioritize safe spaces over the Socratic method. Republican billionaires could fund activist groups that rank universities based on an *academic diversity scale*. When provided reliable analytics, why would any traditional parent send their kids to indoctrination camps and cult-like learning environments? We are not living in the last century where young adults experimented with liberalism in college, graduated, and later found their senses about the limitations of human nature. Today's Marxist diehards are in it for the long haul. Some radicalized daughters would rather become lesbians than be *subservient* to any husband or a future male boss. And our sons may never escape the guilt that comes with being *perpetually privileged*. Why would any traditional parent aspire to do all the right things for the first eighteen years, and then send their child to what is essentially a *cult*?

"Squeezing" radical college professors from every angle could cut off the money that funds the cancer in our divorce. In addition, putting the mass-movement bullseye on the professors and their enablers in pop culture could result in more *intellectuals* and celebrities finding the confidence to break ranks with their colleagues. Is it possible this type of "transfer of allegiance" could result in another *emperor has no clothes* moment in American society?"[cliv] Could a second-term Trump unmask our devil without having to break up the country?

The goal of a continued Trump presidency would be about pushing buttons that can flush out the progressive toxins with the least amount of pain. There is a chance more people will wake up to the brainwashing that is occurring at our universities. But it is also possible it is simply too late to stop the Marxist contagion without a more powerful set of revolutionary tactics.

Eric Hoffer wrote: "Every great cause begins as a movement, becomes a business, and eventually degenerates into a racket."[clv] America was founded on a powerful set of ideas that have been diluted to the point of almost being irrelevant. The United States has become a *big racket* with nearly everyone taking and few giving back. If Trump is reelected, he may find that he needs to do more than just picking fights with academia. Trump may have to move the battle lines closer to those Americans who had a little too much college and not enough real-world observation.

Assuming societal tensions escalated under a post-2020 presidency, Donald Trump would seek to leverage civil unrest to his mass-movement advantage. Angry and emboldened

Blacks and Marxist Whites/Browns will likely overplay their hands. The rioters are not disciplined, organized, and unified by a lasting cause. How does an *agitator-in-chief* president use this reality to his advantage? By allowing the protesters to move closer to suburban areas where professional Whites reside. Much of this sheltered voting bloc has not seen the true intentions of Black Lives Matter. Nor have they seen the anarchy that follows Marxist takeovers. These *educated* Americans have been duped into believing they are privileged because they have white skin and were fortunate enough to have been raised by decent parents.

Why not let college-educated millennial Whites get a taste of the reality that comes with living up close and personal with those who are *not* so privileged? The same with educated Asians and Latinos. Why not let these newcomers see what a United States being managed by Black Lives Matter and Occupy Wall Street will look like should traditional Americans no longer have a voice in societal affairs?

The problem today is that millions of voters haven't figured out that words like *social justice, privilege, and racism* go well beyond instances of White cops making deadly decisions with Black citizens. The broader leftist movement is not about fixing law-enforcement; the real goal is to exploit isolated instances of police injustice into a future movement that destroys the power structure of traditional Whites.

A second-term Trump would also consider standing down and letting blue-state violence pressure liberal governors and mayors into the unenviable position of having to confront their own radical constituencies. By being able to allow leftist anarchy on his own terms, Trump would have the potential to *re-educate the educated* Democrat voters, into understanding that the right type of education matters in a democracy.

What happens if there is no such *traditional awakening* in US society?

If today's acrimony and division escalated under a second-term presidency, Trump should consider the radical idea of giving guilt-ridden Whites, angry Blacks, and undecided Browns their own land. Under this type of scenario, Trump would go back to our previous idea of openly discussing the possibility of agreeing to disagree, and simply asking both sides to sit down and hammer out a resolution that considers breaking up the country by geography. It is possible Trump could push this idea in the context of an Article V convention and become *a mediator-in-chief.* Just as it is possible Trump could strategically allow the country to flounder into widespread civil unrest and then ask the US military to make some very difficult decisions.

In 2013, Detroit became the largest US city to declare Chapter 9 bankruptcy.[clvi] This was a shock to the thousands of people who never contemplated a scenario in which basic services and pension commitments could be wiped away at a moment's notice. The Michigan governor had to appoint a single, unelected official to completely clean house. An *emergency manager* had arbitrary power to void retirement plans, union contracts, public education compacts, and even decisions made by an active and elected city council. For nearly two years, a major American city lost its democratic rights. The emergency manager had the power to give "haircuts" to nearly every financial stakeholder. The problems were so deep, *a dictator* was essentially required to restore order to nearly every facet of life in Detroit.

With Detroit's bankruptcy, everyone initially complained about the haircuts:

- the voters
- the bond holders
- the pensioners
- and the elected City Council.

Thousands of people were angry that a governor and an emergency manager could have so much arbitrary power in a democratically bound city. There were protests. There were racist insults hurled at the Republican governor who *dared* to interfere in Detroit's business. But in the end, everyone got over things, and the books were balanced in Detroit.[clvii]

What does Detroit mean to our discussion today? It may be possible that no elected official will be able to fix the debt and division in the United States. Like Detroit, the US may one day require its own *emergency manager* to fix our broken democracy.

Donald Trump understood the rules of the game had to change in 2016. Four years later, I suspect he understands there is little possibility to balance the books without risking widespread civil unrest. Trump also knows the leftist crazies and anarchists will not be defeated through conventional means. Yes, a second-term Trump should keep attacking college professors, the media, and Hollywood in guerilla-like style. Maybe these groups can be marginalized under a bigger microscope. But a post-2020 Donald Trump should also consider asking a sympathetic group of Joint Chiefs of Staff members to contemplate a take-over scenario on their home field.

Should Trump, or another future president, publicly declare the country is broken beyond democratic repair? Should an American president set the stage for a future *coup by* purging enemies and empowering friends inside the military? And if so, how would such a set of undemocratic circumstances play out in the USA? It's time to begin our closing arguments for the unthinkable idea of using a *temporary* emergency manager to repair our ailing country.

Chapter 13: An American Dictator

If you know the enemy and know yourself, you need not fear the result of a hundred battles. If you know yourself but not the enemy, for every victory gained you will suffer a defeat. If you know neither the enemy nor yourself, you will succumb in every battle.

—*Legendary Sun Tzu*

Whether Donald Trump remains in our divorce conversation or not, there exists a chance the United States will need to *temporarily* set aside its Constitution. If the US doesn't solve its dual problems of debt and dysfunction in a relatively short order of time, Americans from both the left and right may eventually demand a dictator, autocrat, or *emergency manager* to completely clean house and balance the books. This is who we are as human beings; and this is what the academic elites don't seem to understand about human nature. Everyone loves freedom when things are going well, but when presented a choice between chaotic freedom or orderly governance, people will eventually choose order over freedom—even if it means compromising civil liberties in the short run. I don't want to see a dictator in America, but this discussion brings us back to perhaps the three most important questions in the book:

- Under what set of circumstances would the US military break its nonpartisan ranks to lead a reboot of a dysfunctional and broken American democracy?

- At what point would the public be willing to consider its own emergency manager to fix the dysfunction in Washington, D.C?

- If the US broke into two countries, which *side* would the military *align* with?

This last question may be the most important of all. Should blue- and red-Americans not find a way to come together soon, the final arbiter of truth and justice may reside in the Pentagon. The US military has contingency plans for every type of existential threat. Not only are they the best in the world at conducting war, they are also the most respected institution because they do their job well and avoid political gamesmanship. But have our military elites ever contemplated the logistical, political, and cultural ramifications of a *domestic divorce*?

While I don't have an insider's view, I suspect our military leaders understand the future ramifications associated with a broken democracy in conjunction with an emerging China. And if what I witnessed as a military sub-contractor is playing out on the battlefield, the fanatical bureaucrats and PC police are destroying the Warrior spirit. By the end of my contracting career, I couldn't handle the nonsense that came with procuring and managing military work: finding opportunistic minority firms to partner with, the endless bureaucracy, and the rampant political correctness. It was as if completing a job the right way was of least priority. Everything seemed to be about satisfying the PC bureaucracy.

If what I personally experienced working on the military bases here at home is happening in real combat situations, at what point does a decorated group of patriots start asking some hair-raising questions:

- Is the US democracy broken beyond repair?
- What domestic conditions would trigger the military to step in and take *temporary* control of running the US government?
- What would be the national security ramifications if the United States broke into two separate countries?
- Assuming the country broke into two nations, which side would control the nuclear arsenal?

During the Civil War, military men who fought together for years broke ranks to join the Confederate and Union armies. Would such a repeat set of circumstances play out in a *second civil war*? Or would an overwhelming majority of the military align with *red* over *blue*?

How could anyone high up the military chain of command call themselves a Democrat today? We are no longer talking about the era of the Andrew Jackson and Harry S. Truman Democrats. We are living in an era where the progressive core values are based on a world without borders, police, and nation-states. How can active military commanders align with the leftist crazies without first having to *hate themselves*?

How many more monuments of Grant and Lee (and Jackson and Truman) must be destroyed before some very important people break their code of silence? And, perhaps most profoundly, at what point will the Doers, Haves, and Warriors realize they have the *power, guns, and money* to stop the haters and anarchists before it is too late? At what point will the merchant and the Marine align and say, "Enough is enough?"

We don't have the answers to some very important mass-movement questions. We can only speculate that if things got

167

ugly, most military elites would align with a *Red America*. To what extent, we don't know. But if this assumption is wrong, our entire mass-movement strategy could come crashing down. Let's listen to Crane Brinton on how important the military is to a revolutionary movement:

> No revolutionists have ever succeeded until they got a predominance of effective armed forces on their side. This holds true from spears and arrows to machine guns and gas, from Hippias to Castro.[clviii]

We have learned from Trump's experiment of bringing Democrat generals into the White House that military valor doesn't always translate into seeing the whole battlefield. Thus, there exists the chance the military could align with a future Blue America.

If this type of outcome were to be verifiable, the traditionalist patriot should consider standing down and aborting any plans for a future mass movement. If Brinton is right about the revolutionary significance of the military, it is therefore possible the outcome of any *ugly divorce* could be a predetermined defeat.

I'm not sure if our future mass-movement leader would come from the military, or the civilian world, but in the context of a revolutionary environment, this individual would have to command a level of insight, diplomacy, and leadership that is perhaps only found on a once-every-hundred years basis. In what would have to be an impeccably timed decision, this next George Washington or Abraham Lincoln would have to contemplate moral and political dilemmas no less profound than what occurred in the 1770s and 1860s.

According to Eric Hoffer, it would be around this time the "active stage" of the movement would begin. To the public, the *active stage* could be thought of as that succinct "Boston Tea Party" moment when the masses "kick the bums out" and start over. Unlike the agitation period of a mass movement, which can go on for years, the active stage should be short and concise.[clix] As Hoffer explains, "No mass movement, however sublime its fate and worthy in purpose, can be good if its active stage is overlong..."[clx]

This logic makes sense. If there were to be a radical transfer of power to a temporary dictator, Americans would never tolerate an open-ended "dictatorship." They would want to know what the *undemocratic* plan is, how long it will take, and how much pain there will be. And unlike citizens of most other countries, we would hold onto our guns throughout the entire process.

During the active phase of a revolutionary environment, the *temporary dictator* would seek to meet with every aggrieved group: Blacks, Browns, Whites, Republicans, Democrats, business and industry, unions, the universities, and many others. And just like the Detroit bankruptcy in 2013, a team of CPAs and auditors would comb through every dollar of federal debt and future financial obligation. In the best of outcomes, "haircuts" would be given across the board, new coalitions would form, and the country would be put back onto a stable political and financial footing.

In the worst of circumstances, unpredictable violence, forced relocations of millions of people, and new borders would be possible. Under both paths, every fault line would be under review including race relations, citizenship, taxation, debt, bloated bureaucracies, the environment, education, and the specific terms of a possible geographical breakup.

But what about foreign policy? Would countries like China and Iran be able to capitalize off of a broken United States? This question leads us to one last fault line. Eric Hoffer wrote that the ideal, mass-movement "devil" is a foreigner.[clxi] Should a country like China overplay its stealth intentions, is it possible America could finally find a catalyst powerful enough to unite blue- and red-Americans? Let's listen to Hoffer:

> Common hatred unites the most heterogeneous elements. To share a common hatred, with an enemy even, is to infect him with a feeling of kinship, and thus sap his powers of resistance.[clxii]

The Western elites were wrong in assuming a market-reformed China would naturally merge into a democracy. Politicians on both sides are scrambling to catch up to the reality that the US and China may be heading on a future collision course. Nearly two-thirds of the public now have an unfavorable view of China.[clxiii] Each day, more and more Americans are waking up to the possibility of a clash of civilizations.

Are human beings better served with the fast-moving hand of a Chinese autocrat? Or is the slow and sometimes inefficient self-governance style of the Americans the gold standard in human affairs? In a healthy and vibrant society, these types of questions would have already been debated at our universities. Yet in this era of one-sided intellectualism, these types of inconvenient questions go against the prevailing progressive wisdom that *human beings are getting closer to embarking on a future path of open borders, widespread equality, and universal outcomes.*

Should China or another hostile adversary provoke the United States at a time of crisis, could Americans come together like they did after 9/11/2001? Possibly. But probably not for long. It is difficult to come together with a partner who hates everything about their original wedding vows. After 9/11, I paid close attention to the professors, and it was almost as if they were happy *America got what it deserved.*

How can there be any future reconciliation when one side of the marriage has so much hatred for its holidays, monuments, and traditions?

I really don't want to suggest this next thought, but does the possibility exist the "American Way" could one day lose out to the "Chinese Way"? Today, autocrats in countries like China look at our dysfunction and say to their masses, "Look how bad and inefficient the Western democracies are." And at this moment in time, the Chinese are *correct* in their observations.

In the long run, however, there is no way an autocratic civilization can compete against another way of life that attracts people with benevolence. How long can nine men play the shell game of painting individual liberty, freedom of the press, and due process as a bad thing?

Only as long as the United States remains a divided and dysfunctional country.

In this sense, a *healthy United States* will always pose an existential threat to the Politburo and other dictatorships like it. To keep their power in the long run, the Chinese elites need us to be more dysfunctional than they are. This may explain why their government plants spies in our colleges.[clxiv] The Chinese want to assist the *American* professors in casting doubt that the US is an *exceptional* country.

Edmund Burke opined in the eighteenth century that history is a pact between the dead, the living, and the unborn.[clxv] Today, America has lost its ability to harmonize its past with a hopeful future. We no longer admire great heroes from the past because they are guilty of being White and privileged. We indoctrinate the living with pseudo-intellectualism, the politics of victimology, and class envy, and we continue to pile debt onto the unborn. We have become an ignorant and self-indulged civilization in desperate need of a wakeup call.

I began writing *An American Divorce* in 2015. At that time, my friends and family thought I was crazy to write a *revolutionary book* about America. Revolution in the United States? How could this ever happen? My friends and co-workers thought I had ventured into some faraway right-wing crazy land.

My friends and colleagues don't feel this way today.

I'm not sure how far our crystal ball will go in a world with so little predictability. This book was never meant to be a precise roadmap with exact reference points. Rather, the goal was to simply initiate a new conversation, free from the fear and judgment of the twenty-first-century thought police.

I hope it's not too late to bury the ugly monster that grew out of academia. I don't understand why "common-sense" Democrats haven't figured out they will be next in line should the traditionalist fall. Twentieth-century Republicans eventually expunged their fascist moment in the 1950s with Joseph McCarthy. What is stopping *moderate* Democrats from doing the same today?

Most profoundly, why can't the Democrats and Republicans come together to defeat a common enemy that is potentially more ruthless than our worst foreign adversary?

America is an exceptional civilization because it offers hope and optimism that can be aggressively defended from tyrants. For centuries, foreign foes assumed free people would become too decadent to defend themselves. And each time, we proved them wrong. No, we are not perfect as a country; sometimes we are the big elephant in the room that knocks everything down out of naïve intentions; sometimes we simply elect bad presidents who make terrible decisions. But even with our imperfections, the US is a great country that aspires to do good things for the world.

The intellectuals and artists have put our country into an unnecessary state of self-hatred and doubt. Maybe the hatred I witnessed at the university is rooted in arrogance. It must be difficult to be so enlightened and yet live in a country where a bricklayer with a sixth-grade education can make more money than *an intellectual* with a PhD in philosophy.

I *hate* what the professors have done to our great country. I am willing to risk my personal and professional reputation to defeat them. But hate is not the right path to moving away from a toxic relationship; and this reality takes us back to the first quotation in the book:

> When two people decide to get a divorce, it isn't that they don't understand one another, but a sign that they have, at last, begun to.[clxvi]

Hopefully, both sides can now begin to understand their marriage in a deeper context than before. Maybe this understanding will have the potential to avoid a divorce, or at the very least, make any future breakup a little less painful. America can't remain in a state of limbo as a global superpower for much longer. Our unhappy marriage is not fair to the rest of the world. The hatred and division must end, even if the result means breaking up the United States into two separate countries.

As to potential adversaries like China and Iran: be careful what you wish for. If American patriots find a way to defeat the tyranny found in their own backyards, Chinese and Iranian patriots may follow the same revolutionary path in cities like Beijing and Tehran.

I want to close our discussion by again quoting Edmund Burke. This *man of words* famously warned of the tragic consequences when good people hide in the face of tyranny and fascism: "The only thing necessary for the triumph of evil is for good men to do nothing."[clxvii] We know from hindsight what followed Burke's dire warning. The nineteenth-century do-gooder intentions in France led to the Reign of Terror and Napoleon Bonaparte.

As Americans, we are not destined to follow the leftist path of extremism that always seems to lead to dictators and death squads. If we can find ourselves again as a country, the *American way* will be the winner in today's global contest. Dictatorial fear and oppression will never outlast democratic hope and liberty. That is, unless the defenders of liberty stay locked in a perpetual state of guilt, apathy, and paralysis and simply choose to do nothing.

Bibliography

[i] Brooks, David. "The Morality of Selfism." *New York Times: Opinion*,

[ii] "Population estimates, quarterly." *Statistics Canada*. Last modified June 23, 2020. https://doi.org/10.25318/1710000901-eng.

[iii] "Vietnam War Casualties." *The New York Times*, January 24, 1973.

[iv] Obama, Barack. "Obama Campaign Fundraiser." Speech, San Francisco, CA, April 6, 2008.

[v] Hoffer, Eric. *The True Believer*. New York: Perennial, 2002.

[vi] Friedman, Milton. Interview by Phil Donahue. *Donahue*, Multimedia Inc., 1979.

[vii] LeTourneau, Nancy. "Hillary Clinton, Barack Obama and Saul Alinsky." *Washington Monthly*, March 15, 2016.

[viii] Alinsky, Saul. *Rules for Radicals*. Random House, 1971.

[ix] Marx, Karl and Frederich Engels. *The Communist Manifesto*. Translated by Samuel Moore. London: Workers' Educational Association, 1888.

[x] Counting Stars. "The More Than 100 Million Deaths That Communism Caused, Divided by Countries." Last Modified: December 18, 2017. https://www.outono.net/elentir/2017/12/18/the-more-than-100-million-deaths-that-communism-caused-divided-by-countries/.

[xi] Tancredo, Thomas G. *In Mortal Danger: The Battle for America's Border and Security*. Nashville: WND Books, 2006.

[xii] Tanzi, Alex and Vincent Del Giudice. "U.S. Suicide Rate Up 30% Since Start of 21st Century." *Bloomberg*, June 13, 2018. https://www.bloomberg.com/news/articles/2018-06-14/u-s-suicide-rate-up-30-since-start-of-21st-century-cdc-data.

[xiii] *A Guide to Education and No Child Left Behind*. U.S Department of Education, 2004.

[xiv] Skinner, Rebecca and Jody Feder. "Common Core State Standards: frequently asked questions." *CRS Report; R43728* (2018). Accessed: April 2020.

[xv] Patrick, John. "Democratic professors outnumber Republicans 9 to 1 at top colleges." *Washington Examiner*, January 23, 2020.

https://www.washingtonexaminer.com/opinion/democratic-professors-outnumber-republicans-9-to-1-at-top-colleges.

[xvi] Brinton, Crane. *The Anatomy of Revolution*. New York: Random House, 1965.

[xvii] Chen, Grace. "Is Detroit Failing Its Students? Test Scores Say Yes" *Public School Review*, December 23, 2012

[xviii] Obama, Barack. "President Barack Obama." Interviewed by Marc Maron. WTF Podcast, June 22, 2015. Audio, 45:00. http://www.wtfpod.com/podcast/episodes/episode_613_-_president_barack_obama.

[xix] Election Results. *Charter Counter of Wayne Michigan*. Accessed July 17, 2020. https://www.waynecounty.com/elected/clerk/election-results.aspx.

[xx] Isaacson, Walter. "Benjamin Franklin Joins the Revolution." *Smithsonian Magazine*, July 31, 2003. https://www.smithsonianmag.com/history/benjamin-franklin-joins-the-revolution-87199988/.

[xxi] "Census of Population: 1950 Volume II Characteristics of the

Population." *United States Census Bureau*,1950 § (1953).

https://www.census.gov/library/publications/1953/dec/population-vol-

02.html.

[xxii] Mack, Julie. "Which Michigan county ranks No. 1 in births to unmarried

women?" *MLive,* May 20, 2019.

[xxiii] Higgins, Lori. "M-STEP results for Detroit: EAA's overall proficiency

less than 5%" *Detroit Free Press,* August 30, 2016.

[xxiv] McLanahan, Sara. "The Consequences of Single Motherhood." *The

American Prospect*, December 19, 2001.

[xxv] Irving, Shelley K. and Tracy A. Loveless. "Dynamics of Economic

Well-Being: Participation in Government Programs, 2009-2012: Who Gets

Assistance?" 2015.

[xxvi] "Criminal Justice Fact Sheet." NAACP, Accessed: April 2020.

[xxvii] Chaudry, Ajay, Christopher Wimer, Suzanne Macartney, Lauren

Frohlich, Colin Campbell, Kendall Swenson, Don Oellerich, and Susan

Hauan, "Poverty in the United States: 50-Year Trends and Safety Net Impacts." 2016.

xxviii "2018 Crime in the United States: Expanded Homicide Data Table 6," FBI: UCR. Accessed June, 2020. Ucr.fbi.gov.

xxix Reynolds, David S. "Rescuing the Real Uncle Tom." *The New York Times*, June 13, 2011.

xxx Fitzgerald, Maggie. "Black and Hispanic unemployment is at a record low." *CNBC,* October 4, 2019.

xxxi Chaudry, Ajay, Christopher Wimer, Suzanne Macartney, Lauren Frohlich, Colin Campbell, Kendall Swenson, Don Oellerich, and Susan Hauan, "Poverty in the United States: 50-Year Trends and Safety Net Impacts." 2016.

xxxii Wolf, Zachary B. "Here's What the Green New Deal Actually Says." *CNN,* March 2, 2020.

xxxiii Holtz-Eakin, Douglas, Dan Bosch, Ben Gitis, Dan Goldbeck, and Philip Rossetti. "The Green New Deal: Scope, Scale, and Implications." *American Action Forum,* February 25, 2019.

[xxxiv] Fowler, Jack. "What Obama Didn't Say." *National Review*, July 22, 2013.

[xxxv] Ellison, Ralph and John F. Callahan. *Invisible Man*. London: Penguin Books, 2016.

[xxxvi] "Black Student College Graduation Rates Remain Low, But Modest Progress Begins to Show." *The Journal of Blacks in Higher Education*, June 23, 2020. Jbhe.com.

[xxxvii] King, Martin Luther Jr. "I Have a Dream." Speech, Washington, DC, August 28, 1963.

[xxxviii] "U.S. Census Bureau QuickFacts: United States." *Census Bureau QuickFacts*, Accessed: April, 2020.

[xxxix] "Howard Hughes Dies at 70 On Flight to Texas Hospital." *The New York Times*, April 6, 1976.

[xl] "U.S. Census Bureau QuickFacts: United States." *Census Bureau QuickFacts*. Accessed April, 2020.

[xli] "CNN Politics." *CNN Politics*, November 23, 2016.

xlii Mogahed, Dalia and Youssef Chouhoud. "American Muslim Poll 2017: Muslims at the Crossroads." *SSRN Electronic Journal,* 2017.

xliii "U.S. Census Bureau QuickFacts: United States." Census Bureau QuickFacts. Accessed April, 2020.

xliv "Most Dangerous Countries in the World 2020." World Population Review. Accessed July 17, 2020. https://worldpopulationreview.com/country-rankings/most-dangerous-countries

xlv Reilly, Katie. "Here Are All the Times Donald Trump Insulted Mexico." *Time,* August 31, 2016.

xlvi Reilly, Katie. "Here Are All the Times Donald Trump Insulted Mexico." *Time,* August 31, 2016.

xlvii Gonzalez-Barrera, Ana and Jens Manuel Krogstad. "What We Know about Illegal Immigration from Mexico." *Pew Research Center,* June 28, 2019.

xlviii Lipka, Michael. "Muslims and Islam: Key Findings in the U.S. and around the World." *Pew Research Center,* August 9, 2017.

xlix "The World's Muslims: Religion, Politics and Society." *Pew Research Center*, April 30, 2013. Pewforum.org.

l Abulafia, Anna Sapir. "The Abrahamic Religions." *The British Library,* December 7, 2018.

li "Sunnis and Shia: Islam's Ancient Schism." *BBC News,* January 4, 2016.

lii "Muhammad: Legacy of a Prophet. Life of Muhammad." *PBS.* 2002.

liii The Qur'an. [Sahih International, 2:275-279].

liv The Qur'an. [Sahih International, 9:29].

lv The Editorial Board. "Visas for Hong Kong." *The Wall Street Journal*, May 30, 2020. Wsj.com.

lvi The Editorial Board. "Visas for Hong Kong." *The Wall Street Journal*, May 30, 2020. Wsj.com.

lvii Sales, Ben. "America's 7.5 million Jews are older, whiter and more liberal than the country as a whole." *Jewish Telegraphic Agency,* October 7, 2019.

[lviii] "An examination of the 2016 electorate, based on validated voters." *Pew Research Center*, August 9, 2018.

[lix] Wang, Wendy. "The Link Between a College Education and a Lasting Marriage." *Pew Research Center*, December 2, 2015.

[lx] Reilly, Katie. "Read Hillary Clinton's 'Basket of Deplorables' Remarks About Donald Trump Supporters." *Time*, September 10, 2016.

[lxi] Associated Press. "Bush offers up 'ownership society.'" *NBC News*, February 2, 2002. http://www.nbcnews.com/id/6902224/ns/politics-state_of_the_union/t/bush-offers-ownership-society/#.XwS23ShKiBs.

[lxii] Zarroli, Jim. "The U.S. Was Already Deep in Debt. This Year's Deficit Will Be 'Mind Boggling'." *NPR*, March 30, 2020.

[lxiii] Chappel, Bill. "Supreme Court Declares Same-Sex Marriage Legal in All 50 States." *NPR*, June 26, 2015.

[lxiv] "Gender Nation Glossary." *Refinery29*, June 1, 2018. https://www.refinery29.com/en-us/lgbtq-definitions-gender-sexuality-terms.

[lxv] Baculinao, Eric. "Why Is China Raising the Prospect of Same-Sex Marriage?" *NBC News*, January 7, 2020.

[lxvi] Lewis, Sophie. "Putin Wants to Ban Gay Marriage in a Revised Version of the Russian Constitution." *CBS News,* March 3, 2020.

[lxvii] *Obergefell v. Hodges*, 576 U.S. 644 (2015).

[lxviii] *Obergefell v. Hodges*, 576 U.S. 644 (2015).

[lxix] Rudgard, Olivia. "Only Two Thirds of Generation Z Identify as 'Exclusively Heterosexual'." *The Telegraph,* July 4, 2018.

[lxx] Wilhelm, Amara Das. "A Timeline of Gay World History." *GALVA-108,* April 14, 2020.

[lxxi] "The truth about sexuality in ancient Greece and Rome." *Gay Star News,* October 1, 2016. https://www.gaystarnews.com/article/truth-about-sexuality-ancient-greece-and-rome261012/.

[lxxii] Strachan, Maxwell. "The Behind-The-Scenes Story of 'Brokeback Mountain,' 10 Years Later." *HuffPost,* December 11, 2015.

[lxxiii] Elnaiem, Mohammed. "In the McCarthy Era, to Be Black Was to Be Red." *JSTOR Daily,* November 13, 2019. https://daily.jstor.org/in-the-mccarthy-era-to-be-black-was-to-be-red/.

[lxxiv] Lim, Kay M. and Julie Kracov. "The Lavender Scare: How the Federal Government Purged Gay Employees." *CBS News,* June 9, 2019.

[lxxv] Anderson, Hans Christian. *The Emperor's New Clothes.* C.A. Reitzel, 1837.

[lxxvi] Harvey, Matt. "Sen. Joe McCarthy's Startling Morphine Source." *The Fix,* May 13, 2013.

[lxxvii] Harvey, Matt. "Sen. Joe McCarthy's Startling Morphine Source." *The Fix,* May 13, 2013.

[lxxviii] Schlesinger, Arthur Meier. *The Coming of the New Deal, 1933-1935.* Boston: Houghton Mifflin, 2003.

[lxxix] Schlesinger, Arthur Meier. *The Coming of the New Deal, 1933-1935.* Boston: Houghton Mifflin, 2003.

[lxxx] Davis, Alyssa and Lawrence Mishel. "CEO Pay Continues to Rise as Typical Workers Are Paid Less." *Economic Policy Institute,* June 12, 2014.

[lxxxi] Davis, Alyssa and Lawrence Mishel. "CEO Pay Continues to Rise as Typical Workers Are Paid Less." *Economic Policy Institute,* June 12, 2014.

lxxxii Elliot, Larry. "World's 26 Richest People Own as Much as Poorest 50%, Says Oxfam." *The Guardian,* January 21, 2019.

lxxxiii Elkins, Kathleen. "Here's How Much Americans Have Saved for Retirement at Different Ages." *CNBC,* January 23, 2020.

lxxxiv Snider, Susannah. "Tax-Filing in 2020: What is My Tax Bracket?" *U.S. News & World Report,* November 8, 2019.

lxxxv "Topic No. 409 Capital Gains and Losses." *Internal Revenue Service,* February 11, 2020.

lxxxvi Fletcher, Christine. "Eight Things You Need to Know About The Death Tax Before You Die." *Forbes Magazine,* May 20, 2019.

lxxxvii "SEC Adopts Rule for Pay Ratio Disclosure." *U.S. Securities and Exchange Commission*, August 5, 2015. https://www.sec.gov/news/pressrelease/2015-160.html.

lxxxviii "Remarks by the President at a Campaign Event in Roanoke, Virginia." *National Archives and Records Administration*, July 13, 2012.

lxxxix Harris, Ainsley. "Jeff Bezos Made 1.2 Million Times the Median Amazon Employee in 2017." *Fast Company,* April 19, 2018.

[xc] Rogers, Taylor Nicole. "Wealth Tax Explainer: Why Bernie Sanders, Elizabeth Warren and Billionaires like George Soros Alike Are Calling for a Specialized Tax on the Ultra-Wealthy." *Business Insider,* September 24, 2019.

[xci] Rogers, Taylor Nicole. "Wealth Tax Explainer: Why Bernie Sanders, Elizabeth Warren and Billionaires like George Soros Alike Are Calling for a Specialized Tax on the Ultra-Wealthy." *Business Insider,* September 24, 2019.

[xcii] Rogers, Taylor Nicole. "Wealth Tax Explainer: Why Bernie Sanders, Elizabeth Warren and Billionaires like George Soros Alike Are Calling for a Specialized Tax on the Ultra-Wealthy." *Business Insider,* September 24, 2019.

[xciii] Byrnes, Hristina. "U.S. Leads Among Countries That Spend the Most on Public Health Care." *USA Today*, April 11, 2019.

[xciv] Coppess, Jonathan. "1930s Dust Bowl: Government Policy Climate Farming Methods." *AgFax,* October 25, 2019.

[xcv] French, Sally. "The Huge Floating Island of Trash in the Pacific Ocean Is Now Twice the Size of Texas." *MarketWatch,* March 23, 2018.

[xcvi] Newport, Frank. "Americans Greatly Overestimate Percent Gay, Lesbian in U.S." *Gallup,* May 21, 2015.

[xcvii] "Red" states are defined as U.S. states who voted for Donald Trump in 2016. "Blue" states are defined as U.S. states who voted for Hillary Clinton in 2016.

[xcviii] Muro, Mark and Jacob Whiton. "America Has Two Economies—and They're Diverging Fast." *Brookings,* September 19, 2019.

[xcix] Cummings, Michelle. "Who Are the Givers? The Northeast Subsidizes Federal Spending." *Rockefeller Institute of Government,* January 25, 2019.

[c] Cummings, Michelle. "Who Are the Givers? The Northeast Subsidizes Federal Spending." *Rockefeller Institute of Government,* January 25, 2019.

[ci] Schultz, Laura. "Who Are the Getters? The Federal Workforce and Low-Income States Get the Most." *Rockefeller Institute of Government,* February 1, 2019.

[cii] Schultz, Laura. "Who Are the Getters? The Federal Workforce and Low-Income States Get the Most." *Rockefeller Institute of Government,* February 1, 2019.

[ciii] Schultz, Laura. "Who Are the Getters? The Federal Workforce and Low-Income States Get the Most." *Rockefeller Institute of Government,* February 1, 2019.

[civ] Schultz, Laura. "Who Are the Getters? The Federal Workforce and Low-Income States Get the Most." *Rockefeller Institute of Government,* February 1, 2019.

[cv] Kilgore, Ed. "Trump Tax Bill Hammers New York and California." *Intelligencer, New York Magazine*, November 2, 2017.

[cvi] "U.S. Census Bureau QuickFacts: Arkansas; Louisiana; Mississippi; United States." *Census Bureau QuickFacts*. Accessed April 2020.

[cvii] "U.S. Census Bureau QuickFacts: Connecticut; Vermont; Massachusetts; United States." *Census Bureau QuickFacts*. Accessed April, 2020.

[cviii] Harrington, John. "There Are 18.2 Million Veterans in the US. Which State Is Home to the Most of Them?" *USA Today,* July 4, 2019.

[cix] Reilly, Katie. "Read Hillary Clinton's 'Basket of Deplorables' Remarks About Donald Trump Supporters." *Time,* September 10, 2016.

[cx] Kelly, Martin. "Which State Seceded First During the American Civil War?" *ThoughtCo.*, February 11, 2019. https://www.thoughtco.com/order-of-secession-during-civil-war-104535.

[cxi] Kelly, Martin. "Which State Seceded First During the American Civil War?" *ThoughtCo.*, February 11, 2019. https://www.thoughtco.com/order-of-secession-during-civil-war-104535.

[cxii] Beckert, Sven. "Empire of Cotton." *The Atlantic,* December 12, 2014.

[cxiii] Hawes, Robert F. *One Nation, Indivisible?: A Study of Secession and the Constitution.* Palo Alto: Fultus Corporation, 2006.

[cxiv] Hawes, Robert F. *One Nation, Indivisible?: A Study of Secession and the Constitution.* Palo Alto: Fultus Corporation, 2006.

[cxv] U.S. Constitution. Article IV. Sec. 3. Cl. 1. https://www.senate.gov/civics/constitution_item/constitution.htm#a4.

[cxvi] Texas v. White, 74 US 700. Supreme Court, 1869.

[cxvii] Rogers, Abby. "Sorry Secessionists, Justice Scalia Won't Help You Out." *Business Insider,* November 15, 2012.

[cxviii] "Article V, U.S. Constitution." *National Archives and Records Administration.* Accessed: May, 2020.

[cxix] U.S. Constitution, Article V. *National Archives.*

[cxx] Coyle, Marcia. "Scalia, Ginsburg Offer Amendments to the Constitution." *National Law Journal*, April 17, 2014.

[cxxi] America's Founding Documents: The Constitution. National Archives, Washington DC. https://www.archives.gov/founding-docs

[cxxii] Moran, Chris. "The Curious Story of the Confederate 'Greyback'." *Greenwich Sentinel*, February 12, 2016.

[cxxiii] Wolf, Stephen. "Daily Kos Election Presents the 2016 Presidential Election Results by Congressional District." *Daily Kos*, January 30, 2017.

[cxxiv] Brinton, Crane. *The Anatomy of Revolution.* New York: Random House, 1965.

[cxxv] Brinton, Crane. *The Anatomy of Revolution.* New York: Random House, 1965.

[cxxvi] Brinton, Crane. *The Anatomy of Revolution.* New York: Random House, 1965.

J. N. Welch

[cxxvii] Hoffer, Eric. *The True Believer.* New York: Perennial, 2002.

[cxxviii] Hoffer, Eric. *The True Believer.* New York: Perennial, 2002.

[cxxix] Hoffer, Eric. *The True Believer.* New York: Perennial, 2002.

[cxxx] Hoffer, Eric. *The True Believer.* New York: Perennial, 2002.

[cxxxi] Hoffer, Eric. *The True Believer.* New York: Perennial, 2002.

[cxxxii] Brinton, Crane. *The Anatomy of Revolution.* New York: Random House, 1965.

[cxxxiii] Brinton, Crane. *The Anatomy of Revolution.* New York: Random House, 1965.

[cxxxiv] Brinton, Crane. *The Anatomy of Revolution.* New York: Random House, 1965.

[cxxxv] Alinsky, Saul. *Rules for Radicals.* Random House, 1971.

[cxxxvi] Frank, Robert. "Hillary is the favorite among millionaire voters: Survey." *CNBC,* May 6, 2015.

[cxxxvii] Alinsky, Saul. *Rules for Radicals.* Random House, 1971.

cxxxviii Brinton, Crane. *The Anatomy of Revolution*. New York: Random House, 1965.

cxxxix Hoffer, Eric. *The True Believer*. New York: Perennial, 2002.

cxl Alinsky, Saul. *Rules for Radicals*. Random House, 1971.

cxli Alinsky, Saul. *Rules for Radicals*. Random House, 1971.

cxlii Alinsky, Saul. *Rules for Radicals*. Random House, 1971.

cxliii Alinsky, Saul. *Rules for Radicals*. Random House, 1971.

cxliv Alcorn, Jonathan. "How Al Gore Amassed a $200 Million Fortune After Presidential Defeat." *Bloomberg*, May 6, 2013.

cxlv Dalton, Sam. "Chelsea Clinton's millions and the American aristocracy." *World Socialist Web Site,* January 10, 2020.

cxlvi Fisher, Anthony L. "Elizabeth Warren's advice to parents of kids in struggling public schools reeks of privilege." *Business Insider*, December 19, 2019.

[cxlvii] Ivanova, Polina, Maria Tsvetkova, Ilya Zhegulev and Luke Baker. "What Hunter Biden did on the board of Ukrainian energy company Burisma." *Reuters*, October 18, 2019.

[cxlviii] Brinton, Crane. *The Anatomy of Revolution.* New York: Random House, 1965.

[cxlix] Parker, Maggie. "The 12 Most Unique College Courses Offered Around the U.S." *Bestlife,* July, 2018.

[cl] Brinton, Crane. *The Anatomy of Revolution.* New York: Random House, 1965.

[cli] Alinsky, Saul. *Rules for Radicals.* Random House, 1971.

[clii] Jurecic, Quinta. "Why the Kavanaugh Confirmation Still Haunts Us." *The Atlantic,* September 18, 2019.

[cliii] Matousek, Mark. "Elon Musk says you still don't need a college degree to work at Tesla. Here's what he looks for in job applicants instead." *Business Insider*, January 8, 2020.

[cliv] Brinton, Crane. *The Anatomy of Revolution.* New York: Random House, 1965.

[clv] Hoffer, Eric. *The True Believer.* New York: Perennial, 2002.

[clvi] Rushe, Dominic. "Detroit becomes largest US city to file for bankruptcy in historic 'low point.'" *The Guardian,* July 18, 2013.

[clvii] Klinefelter, Quinn. "Detroit's Big Comeback: Out of Bankruptcy, A Rebirth." *NPR Morning Edition,* December 18, 2018.

[clviii] Brinton, Crane. *The Anatomy of Revolution.* New York: Random House, 1965.

[clix] Hoffer, Eric. *The True Believer.* New York: Perennial, 2002.

[clx] Hoffer, Eric. *The True Believer.* New York: Perennial, 2002.

[clxi] Hoffer, Eric. *The True Believer.* New York: Perennial, 2002.

[clxii] Hoffer, Eric. *The True Believer.* New York: Perennial, 2002.

[clxiii] Devlin, Kat, Laura Silver, and Christine Huang. "U.S. Views of China Increasingly Negative Amid Coronavirus Outbreak." *Pew Research Center,* April 21, 2020.

[clxiv] Dilanian, Ken. "American universities are a soft target for China's spies, say U.S. intelligence officials." *NBC News,* February 2, 2020.

clxv Burke, Edmund. "Reflections on the Revolution in France," 1790. *The Works of the Right Honorable Edmund Burke,* vol. 3, p. 359 (1899).

clxvi Rowland, Helen. *Reflections of a Bachelor Girl.* New York: Dodge Publishing Company, 1909.

clxvii Attributed to Edmund Burke. "Thoughts on the Cause of the Present Discontents," 82-83 (1770) in: *Select Works of Edmund Burke, vol. 1, p. 146. Liberty Fund edition, 1999.*

Made in the USA
Las Vegas, NV
08 January 2021

15535563R00114